THIS BOOK SHOULD BE RETURNED ON OR BEFORE THE LATEST
DATE SHOWN TO THE LIBRARY FROM WHICH IT WAS BORROWED

AUTHOR	CLASS
CARR, D.	715.1

TITLE
Topiary and plant sculpture

Topiary and Plant Sculpture

TOPIARY & PLANT
SCULPTURE

A Beginner's Step-By-Step Guide

DAVID CARR

The Crowood Press

First published in 1989 by
The Crowood Press
Ramsbury, Marlborough
Wiltshire SN8 2HE

British Library Cataloguing in Publication Data

Carr, David, *1930-*
  Topiary and plant sculpture: a beginner's step-by-step guide.
  1. Gardens. Topiary work
  1. Title
  715:1

  ISBN 1 85223 148 3

Picture Credits
Line illustrations by Sharon Perks
Jacket photographs by Andrew Lawson
All colour photographs by Andrew Lawson,
except Hidcote Manor Gardens by Tim Moore

Typeset by Avonset, Midsomer Norton, Nr Bath, Avon
Printed in Great Britain by The Bath Press

Contents

Introduction

According to popular image and the present-day dictionary definition, topiary can be summed up as 'the art of clipping shrubs into ornamental forms'. Many gardeners would be inclined to substitute 'evergreens' for 'shrubs', but would otherwise go along with this idea. However, limiting the scope to evergreens is a somewhat narrow notion. Similarly, the art is not limited simply to clipping. The word topiary comes from *topiarus* – the Latin word for landscape gardener – and to modern minds this probably implies a much greater field of activity. That is what this book is all about – the wider ramifications; the embracing and gathering together of other and varied forms of plant sculptures, and then the floating of ideas to bring them within the reach of the smaller garden of today.

Topiary has a long history, of 2,000 years and more, and there are examples recorded in the Latin writings of both Pliny the Younger and his uncle, Pliny the Elder. There is also evidence to suggest that topiary skills were practised in Britain in those far-off Roman days, with the results used to set off the villas of the rich to perfection. Once the Romans had left Britain, and for over a thousand years after – until Tudor times, under Henry VIII – topiary seems to have been confined in the main to monastery gardens. From about 1588 and the reign of Queen Elizabeth I, until the reign of Queen Anne in the eighteenth century, the art of topiary really became popular, both in Britain and in Europe – this was its 'golden age'. Figures sculpted in box, rosemary and juniper were much in vogue, and knot gardens, parterres and mazes became highly fashionable in the gardens of large country houses. Several outstanding examples of this early topiary can still be seen today, such as the chessmen at Hever Castle in Kent and the yew creations of Levens Hall in Cumbria, which both date back to around 1750. Surprisingly, yew was not used to any great extent for topiary before this time.

Following this period of enthusiasm, which had begun with the increased wealth of the Renaissance, there was a lull, and for nearly 100 years there was little progress in the art. It was the Victorian era which was to bring an upsurge in interest and activity, and this became a time of change which transformed the scene. New plants were imported from overseas, and an international exchange of ideas and techniques became commonplace.

Two world wars, rising costs, and the breaking up of large estates all discouraged expansion in the first half of the twentieth century. Today, however, the fascinating art of topiary and plant sculptures is once again catching the imagination and the interest of gardeners, who are encouraged in no small way by widespread home ownership, increased know-how, and modern power tools which make the job easier.

INTERNATIONAL ORIGINS

Topiary and plant sculptures are truly international in character, and their international origins are reflected in the terminology surrounding their subject. For example, 'topiary' comes from the Latin, 'espalier' and 'treillage' from the French, 'pleaching' from old English, and so on. Techniques have developed spasmodically through the centuries, and each country's particular style has left its mark. In more recent times, French, Italian and Dutch styles have played a part, as have the unique skills from Japan, China and the Orient. Nowadays, America, living up to her reputation in these matters, is once again leading the way on how to adapt to the changing circumstances of the day.

PLANT SCULPTURES – SOME DEFINITIONS

Topiary This is all about shaping free-standing trees and shrubs into ornamental forms by clipping them with shears. It is still the most widely practised of all the forms of plant sculpture.

Treillage This is the art of growing weak-stemmed vines and other climbing and trailing plants over some form of support – trellis and lattice are particularly useful for this type of work. Having spent a considerable time in the doldrums, treillage is making something of a comeback, especially in the USA.

Pleaching The effects of pleaching can basically be described as 'topiary on stilts'. A fairly typical example would be two lines of uniform trees or hedging, flanking a pathway, with stems or trunks bared for a minimum of 3ft (1m) above soil level. (*Note* The term 'pleaching' is sometimes used, somewhat confusingly, to describe trees or shrubs trained treillage fashion over a pergola to form a covered alleyway.)

Pinch and prune sculptures This term represents the wide umbrella which covers

the formation and care of standards, pyramids, fans, espaliers and cordons. These are familiar terms, by virtue of their everyday usage in intensive fruit growing. One major difference between pinch and prune sculpture and true topiary is the method of treatment. Thumb nails, knives and pruners are used, as opposed to the shearing and clipping action common to topiary. The pinch and prune technique is by far the most rapidly expanding of all forms of plant sculpture. To a large extent, this is due to the adaptation into the ornamental field of lessons learned from intensive fruit growers.

Carpet bedding sculptures This came into being in the Victorian era, and ranks with the youngest and newest of crafts. To perfect the technique, containers are fashioned out of wire netting. They are lined with moss or plastic sheet and filled with potting compost. Small carpet bedding plants are pushed through the moss or plastic until their roots are embedded in moist compost, and living sculptures are created by covering both the sides and the tops of the containers with plants. Given the correct choice of plants, very often little or no pruning is subsequently called for.

PLANT SCULPTURES IN THE GARDEN

Topiary

Topiary can be used in many and varied ways around the garden, but it is most in keeping with a formal, geometric and usually ordered character and style. Be wary of putting too heavy an emphasis on severe angular topiary, however, as the result in a garden is likely to be over-architectural. Also remember that where clipped plain evergreens are allowed to

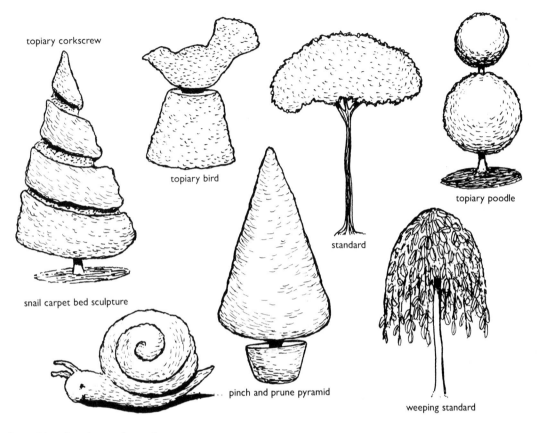

topiary corkscrew

topiary bird

standard

topiary poodle

snail carpet bed sculpture

pinch and prune pyramid

weeping standard

Some ideas for plant sculpture forms.

predominate, there is a tendency for colour to be sparse. If this is a danger, introduce some berrying and variegated topiaries to relieve the monotony and lighten the overall effect. Where time and finances permit, any deficiencies in flower colour can be overcome by planting up with spring and summer bedding in due season. Few would argue that these plants are not at their best set against a backdrop of green.

If a topiary-dominated garden is to be successful, variations in texture, form, shape, light and shade must be exploited. Close-clipped, small-leaved box, juniper and yew will provide a much denser texture than, for example, the larger-leaved bay, holly and elaeagnus. Shape and form are two of the more obvious features and self-explanatory, but perhaps not so self-evident is the interplay of light and shade at different times of day, and at different seasons of the year. Long morning, evening or winter shadows will always provide interesting effects, both on a lawn and on a hard-surfaced area. When silhouetted against an evening or winter sky, topiaries instantly become a talking point in any company, and, for those who are into garden lighting, there is no better subject than a good topiary to flood, spot or back light.

For Enclosure and Division

Strictly speaking, a **clipped hedge** is the most common form of topiary, although it is rarely thought of as such. In the average modern garden, a hedge is invariably a simple and unpretentious green wall boundary, ranging in height from 3–6ft (90–180cm), but much more could be made of it. For example, a hedge can be embellished with **buttresses** and perhaps topped with topiary features. Under these circumstances it is usual to train buttresses at intervals along the hedge, spacing them out in much the same way as if they were being used to strengthen a brick or stone wall. The most suitable features to train for the top come in the form of geometric figures, globes and pyramids, and in country districts, under the guidance of craftsmen, it is not unusual to see animals and birds. When you are planting a new topiary hedge, give some thought to selecting different-coloured foliage shrubs for the infill panels between the buttresses. Green-leaved hedging for the buttresses, contrasted with silver or golden variegated plants for the panels, would make one very good combination.

Another feature which can often be worked into the topiary hedge is the **clipped archway**. This is ideal also for framing attractive views and welcoming visitors.

The high-hedged **maze**, so popular from Tudor times right up to the nineteenth century, really has no comfortable place in the modern garden. However, the practical variant, whereby cubes, rectangles, and 'L'-shaped blocks are cut out of groups of hedging plants, can look quite at home, even in a small town garden. And on the same theme, but on an even smaller scale, clipped blocks of perennial herbs, set amongst paving, are both useful and attractive.

Topiary hedging also has great potential in terms of edgings. Most gardeners are familiar with the use of clipped box, dwarf lavender and similar shrubs to separate paths from beds and borders, but two other ideas from the past which are worth updating to the demands of present-day small gardens, are the **knot garden** and the **parterre**.

knot garden – beds edged with clipped plants

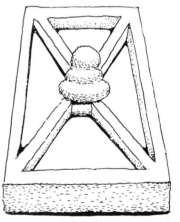

parterre – bed divided into compartments by clipped edging

A knot garden and a parterre compared.

The **knot garden**, a legacy of the Tudor and Jacobean periods of the sixteenth and seventeenth centuries, is a mix of topiary and formality. Very often, four or more self-contained beds were edged around with box or rosemary to create a regular, geometric layout – the main feature common to all. Each bed was separated from its neighbour by a path, and the whole thing was popularly finished off with a clipped topiary centre-piece which frequently took the form of an animal, a corkscrew, a globe or a narrow column. The beds in turn were usually planted with flowers or herbs, and in the eighteenth century it was not unusual for low-growing vegetables such as carrots to be grown alongside the herbs. Occasionally coloured stones would take the place of the plants – this idea may well have originated from Italy where it was commonplace at the time. Today, the re-creation of a knot garden would be especially in keeping with an older-style cottage, but they certainly don't look out of place, scaled down, in a small town front garden either.

The **parterre**, with its French-sounding name, used to consist of one or more beds, broken up into panels or segments, which were divided from each other by low hedging. It was usual to plant up the individual panels with flowers or ground cover of diminutive stature, or to use gravel to fill them in. Parterres were very much in vogue in the fifteenth, sixteenth and seventeenth centuries, but their scale makes them relatively easy to fit into a modern garden. You should not attempt a knot garden or parterre unless you are prepared to clip the low hedging regularly, and this can be very time-consuming and demanding work. Also a problem is the constant necessity to bait the slugs.

For Ornamental Purposes

Topiary is particularly noteworthy and valuable for its decorative garden effects, and there are a few basic ideas which can be adapted to suit the purposes of your own garden.

Wall features   Flat wall topiaries (along with espaliers and fans) are excellent for relieving bare expanses of walling. Climbers and wall shrubs come into their own here too, and can be very effective if they are suitably clipped.

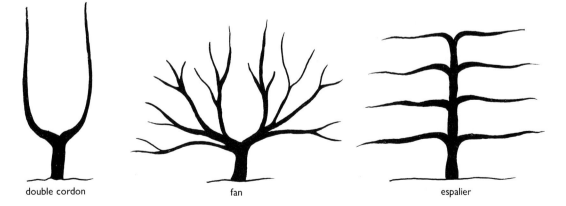

double cordon   fan   espalier

Forms of wall sculpture.

Steps, entrances and doorways These lend themselves to being flanked on either side with pairs of matching topiary features. These can be planted directly in position but are more usually grown in containers. In many instances they make a useful starting point for newcomers to the topiary scene, who can start with clipped columns and globes, before moving on to the more ambitious poodles, spirals and other animal characters.

Focal points A topiary figure, carefully sited, will add interest to an otherwise dull corner, or close a vista at the end of a pathway most effectively. It can also be used to replace a specimen tree or shrub in most instances.

Topiary gardens These should only be considered by the dedicated topiarist and plant sculpturist with the time, interest and commitment to succeed, and the patience to wait for the garden to come to fruition. A small container-grown poodle, for instance, will take at least seven years, and probably longer, to complete, starting with a well-developed bush with a moderate to fast growth rate. The work is not necessarily hard or onerous, but regular attention to detail is required. A lawn is a fairly popular place to create a topiary garden, and the easiest is probably one of globes, cubes and poodle shapes in box or yew. At the risk of repeating myself, a topiary garden on a larger scale is definitely not something to be undertaken lightly, without first making adequate provision for maintenance.

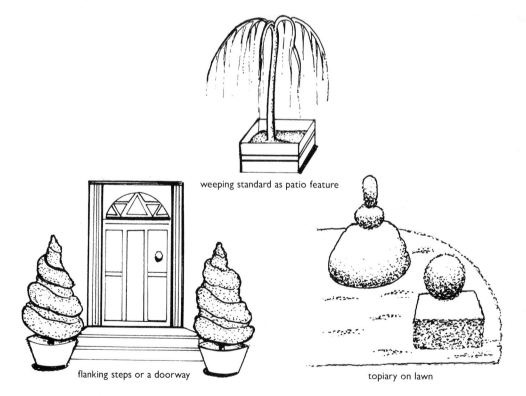

weeping standard as patio feature

flanking steps or a doorway

topiary on lawn

Using and siting plant sculptures to their best advantage.

Pleaching A sheltered, pleached walkway is a variation of the topiary hedge. It is, however, more suited to the larger garden which has sufficient space to absorb a corridor effect.

Pinching and pruning Screens are easily created by training trees and shrubs, and these can be used effectively to separate vegetables from flowers, for example. Cordons, espaliers and fans, grown on free-standing post and wire supports, are suitable for the purpose, and these screens may be of edible fruits or purely ornamental in nature.

A well-grown flowering plant will enliven your patio, balcony or courtyard. Especially noteworthy in this respect are standard or pyramid fuchsias, while a standard cotone-aster can be relied on to put up a brave show with its red berries in autumn and winter. Most of us are familiar with standard ger-aniums used to add height and interest to a display of summer bedding, but how many ever think of using a standard hardy hibiscus for an autumn feature in a mixed shrub bed or border? If spindle, maple and purple beech are trained as standards, they can also be used for colourful foliage effects, in much the same way as the flowering varieties just discussed.

Treillage This is not often seen in Britain, apart from at flower shows, and as window dressings by a few top-class garden centres. Treillage works of arbours and bird cages, clad with climbers, were at one time an important feature of many wealthy gardens and public parks. It is an art which could easily be taken up again today, since with imagination, climber-clad animals, birds and geometric shapes are all possible. Another form of treillage – again, seen less today than formerly – is the training of shrubs over tripods or in columns as a focal point. Roses used to be

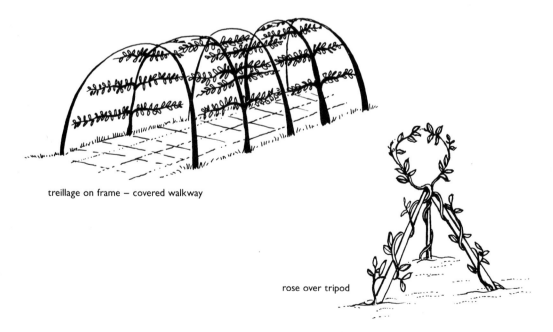

treillage on frame – covered walkway

rose over tripod

Garden features using plants trained over frames.

13

very popular for this purpose, and the more ambitious gardeners would use the tripods as a base for building up wire frames of hearts, chaplets and trefoil leaves.

Carpet bedding Simple frames can be fashioned into letters, hearts and cushions, but it takes some experience to create floral clocks and emblems. Because watering is usually essential, carpet bedding sculptures should be sited within easy reach of a tap! Provided suitable plants are used, carpet bedding sculptures can be made up to decorate the home. Although it is true that many carpet bedding plants are difficult to nurse through winter, many others cause few problems, so don't be put off on this score. (*See* plant guide, page 100.)

Collecting Plant Sculptures

By using your imagination and diligence it is possible to build up impressive collections of plant sculptures in containers, and, there is considerable scope here for the enthusiast to find a hobby of absorbing and lasting interest. Collections can even be built up Bonsai style, in miniature. But do bear in mind, if containers are used, winter shelter from wind, frost, snow and heavy rain is essential, as is shade from direct sun in summer.

Know-how

Simple topiary and plant sculptures are normally within the grasp and capabilities of anyone who is reasonably fit and able, and prepared to set about mastering the art. Given the time, a determination to succeed, steady hands, plus an eye for detail, a modicum of know-how is all that remains to be learned. In the pages which follow the facts are provided, but theory is no real substitute for practical experience and observation, and it is a good idea to get out and about to see some examples of good topiary and plant sculptures. Better still, aim to watch an experienced practitioner at work.

1 Making a Start

It makes good sense to take time at the outset to think things through, so that you develop a clear idea of the likely extent of the work involved. Will it be a case of maintenance only, or are you intending to set up new projects? It is one thing to begin with a ready-made garden with established plant sculptures and topiary features, and quite another to start from scratch. It should be relatively simple to keep a well-grown plant sculpture looking its best, given a few sound guidelines, whereas renovating to improve neglected or damaged features is usually rather more demanding. But the most demanding of all – in terms of time, know-how and expenditure – is training from the beginning. It is highly satisfying work which provides scope for imaginative schemes, but careful planning is certainly called for.

TOOLS AND EQUIPMENT

Once the nature of the workload has been established, a realistic assessment of the necessary tools and equipment can be made. With a little forethought, it should be possible to avoid falling into the trap of buying unnecessarily and cluttering up valuable storage space. Firstly, it is important to decide early on in proceedings if any of the work is to be carried out by contractors. Next, you should look at the practicality of hiring as opposed to buying. Consider hiring expensive items which will be used only infrequently, and take a gamble on their being to hand reasonably promptly – remember that one of the main snags with hiring tools is that they are not always available on demand. Hiring is the obvious answer with such equipment as powered cultivators and earth-moving tools which would probably be used for garden making, and rarely thereafter. The situation is somewhat different when it comes to powered garden trimmers, which are needed for the routine care of topiaries. Most will need clipping several times a year, and it will work out cheaper in the long run to buy rather than hire. And it will certainly be more convenient.

For Maintenance

The basic items of equipment which will form the backbone of your kit for caring for existing trained features are as follows:

Hand pruners – called for in most gardens and not just for topiary. There is not a great deal to choose between the so-called 'anvil' type and the 'bi-pass' models, but one of the main points to watch for is that the pruners are comfortable and of a size to suit the individual concerned.

A sharp knife of the folding or pocket type – stainless steel blades are easier to keep clean and sharp.

Scissors – a strong pair of narrow pointed vine or Bonsai scissors are vital for the very fine work that is involved when dealing with miniature Bonsai and small container plants. Again, stainless steel is preferable.

A straight edge – a straight bamboo cane, or light timber lath of 6ft (1.8m) minimum length, is a boon as a guide for clipping straight tops and sides.

Powered garden clippers – as listed in some catalogues, and alternatively referred to as 'hedge trimmers'. Because of the work involved anyone thinking of taking up topiary seriously should buy a good powered trimmer. They are definitely warranted where the amount of clipping is likely to exceed the equivalent of about 100ft (30m) in length of 5ft (1.5m) high hedge in a year. Electric models are considerably cheaper, lighter in weight, less tiring to use, quieter, and easier to start and run than those which are petrol driven. The disadvantage is that there is the ever-present nuisance of trailing cables, and the subsequent need for extra vigilance against accidental electrocution. Check on the length of cable which will be needed – anything over about 150ft (45m) is heavy to handle and therefore dangerous. In the interests of safety, the use of an electric power breaker is also strongly recommended, to switch off the current automatically if a fault occurs or if the cable is cut. You must make sure, too, that the model you select is not too heavy to use in comfort. These powered clippers come in various cutting widths from 12–30in (30–75cm). Hand shears are the alternative to powered trimmers.

Go for the best you can afford. Under heavy use, those tools at the cheaper end of the range are prone to chewing the vegetation: their handles quickly slacken and the centre pivot soon shows signs of wear.

Donkey sheet – should be strong of about 5ft (1.5m) square, in plastic or fabric with four strong corner handles. It will be extremely useful for spreading out under topiaries before clipping begins – the trimmings are then easily gathered up without the need for raking. It will also be handy for transporting prunings, by simply gathering up the corners.

Miscellaneous – It is assumed that hand tools such as a rake, fork and spade are already to hand, and they will be needed for cleaning up and for planting. A wheelbarrow may not be essential in a small garden, but it makes life a lot easier if there is fetching and carrying to do – where storage space is at a premium, you should consider the folding kind.

For Formation Pruning

For the tools needed for pruning and cutting *see* above. Where new sculptures are envisaged, provision must also be made for support. A combination of stakes and posts, wires and ties, trellis and wall fixings will be needed, depending on the sculpture in question, along with such household items as pliers, a hammer and a screwdriver.

THE GARDEN AS A PLANT HABITAT

Whether you are planning a new layout or improving an existing one, you should always choose plants to suit the site if you want a reasonable chance of good growth.

The Climate

The climate is the most powerful influence likely to affect plant growth and survival. For practical purposes the British Isles can be broadly divided into cold, average and mild climatic regions. Gardens in the cold climate of northern England and Scotland have to endure long, hard winters with severe frosts and very often heavy falls of snow. The frosts start in September and continue late into spring, and only the hardiest of trees and shrubs can be relied on to survive outdoors and give a good display in due season. The mild climate of much of southern England and western coastal areas permits the greatest choice of plants. Many of the more tender varieties will survive the relatively mild winters outdoors. These areas have the longest frost-free period between spring and autumn, making displays of half-hardy perennials very worthwhile. Most of central England has a climate which is somewhere in between those of the cold northern areas and the mild southern and western districts. (The plants listed later in the book are given hardiness ratings which should help you choose.)

Shelter

This exerts a moderating influence on the climate within a garden. For instance, a south- or west-facing wall or fence will give protection from cold north and east winds and make the garden warmer. The significance? It is quite feasible to grow successfully the tender camellia, magnolia, escallonia, piptanthus and olearia in a sheltered garden in what is calculated to be an area with an average climate. The converse is also true. Any garden exposed to cold prevailing winds is likely to be colder than the norm for the area. Gardens of hillsides facing north or east are among the most exposed, and you should make allowances accordingly.

Draughty cold passageways between buildings have a turbulent and cooling effect, and sheltered town gardens tend to be a few degrees warmer than their counterparts in the surrounding countryside – these are other points to watch. Also, in coastal gardens you will need to go for wind-tolerant trees and shrubs.

Frost Pockets

If a garden is susceptible to late spring frosts avoid planting tender early-flowering ornamentals such as peach, plum, cherry, camellia and magnolia. As for half-hardy perennials,

you will have to be prepared to set them out later, and so settle for a shorter flowering season. Completely enclosed gardens, surrounded by non-permeable high walls or fences, can be hazardous when it comes to frost. On calm, clear nights cold air collects at ground level and accumulates rather like water in a pool. A similar thing happens in gardens situated in hollows and valley bottoms, and even southern gardens are at risk if they are situated in those potential frost pockets. In this respect, cold northern gardens are a gamble at best.

On the subject of frost there is one other factor to bear in mind – south and west-facing walls have a warming effect. Sun and heat taken in during the day is given off at night, and this helps to keep wall-trained trees a few degrees warmer, and gives added frost protection in spring.

Light

Sunlight and shade exert a powerful influence on growth. Most gardens are a patchwork of differing light levels, so, before choosing plants, note down which parts of the garden receive full sun for most of the day, which are partially shaded, and which are in permanent shade. Note too the likely seasonal variations between midsummer when shadows are shortest and midwinter as they lengthen.

Open **south-facing aspects**, which are not overshadowed by nearby buildings and the like, normally provide the sunniest sites where most flowering trees and shrubs, and half-hardy perennials, will flourish.

Although **west-facing sites** are partially shaded they are kind to, and safe for, almost any plant.

East-facing sites are also shaded for part of the day. However, being open to early morning sun they are treacherous to trees and shrubs which are in leaf or flower in late winter or spring. Morning sun after overnight frost invariably results in blackening and injury to buds and foliage. This is caused by too rapid a thaw. Stick to late-flowering deciduous varieties in these situations.

North-facing aspects are often in permanent shade. Such sunless, cold sites are suitable only for the hardiest of shade-tolerant trees and shrubs, such as Lawson cypress, yew, juniper, holly and mahonia. From the half-hardy herbaceous plants 'busy Lizzie' and 'mind-your-own-business' are two of the safest to choose.

Generally speaking, deciduous broad-leaved flowering trees, shrubs and climbers are light-demanding, as are half-hardy perennials – all these plants need sun. Evergreens will tolerate partial shade, but those with gold, silver, blue or variegated foliage are exceptions to the rule. These will need sun if they are to colour well. Many plants will grow happily under the light-dappled shade of broad-leaved trees such as birch, but the dense overhead canopy of evergreens such as yew and cedar is likely to shut out too much light for any worthwhile underplanting. Similarly, watch out for nearby high buildings – they too can shut out too much light.

The Soil

Most trees, shrubs, climbers and half-hardy perennials will grow satisfactorily in any average, reasonably fertile garden soil. It is when soils are far from average that problems arise and plants start to show their definite preferences.

Knowing what kind of soil makes up the bulk of the garden helps to ensure success since it is then possible to select the right sort of varieties to suit it. Thereafter you can also vary their treatment accordingly, so avoiding mistakes in cultivation, manuring and feeding.

For practical purposes soils are invariably grouped into four types: heavy, medium loam, sandy light and peaty moss.

Heavy clay soils drain slowly and water tends to stand around on them after heavy rain. They are sticky and difficult to work when wet – indeed, no attempt should ever be made to do this. They dry out slowly in spring and are slow to warm up. When dry they set brick-hard and a shrunken, cracked, baked surface is typical in summer.

Medium loam soils are good blends of clay and sand and are close to the ideal. Easy to cultivate, they are moisture and nutritive-retentive.

Sandy light soils are relatively easy to work, but they drain rapidly after heavy rain and dry out quickly in fine weather, to the detriment of plants. Nutrients are soon washed out, hence their reputation as hungry soils.

Peaty moss and **fen** soils are common to the fenlands of eastern England and East Anglia, and to the mossland areas of Lancashire and Cheshire. They are usually dark in colour and spongy in texture, and, provided they are well drained, they present few problems.

Soil Lime Content

This has an important bearing on the ability of many plants to grow and flourish. So before opting for lime-sensitive plants (see plant guide), do a pH test. Use one of the low-cost test kits – the instructions are easy to follow and the results reasonably accurate.

Soil Depth

In order to provide good anchorage and sustain growth, trees need a minimum depth of good topsoil of 18–24in (45–60cm); shrubs 15in (38cm); and herbaceous perennials 10in (25cm).

Drainage

If water lies on the surface for any significant length of time after rain has stopped, the soil obviously needs draining. However, poor drainage is not always evident from the surface. If in doubt, dig out a test hole in a low-lying position during winter. Make it about 18in (45cm) deep and 12in (30cm) square, and cover it with a dustbin lid to keep out the rain. Examine it regularly – if standing water accumulates to a depth of more than 6in (15cm), you should set about draining the land.

BUYING

Where to Obtain Plants

When plant hunting, you should start by looking in garden centres and nurseries where plants can be seen and assessed for quality, and price, before purchase. Buying in plants from a mail order firm, or pre-packed from a centrally-heated shop or store is too much of a gamble. This is especially so in the case of trees and shrubs which are about to have many years of training expended on them. You must steer clear, too, of bargain offers and end-of-season clearance sales for this specialist work. Home-grown plants are fine, provided they are healthy, well cared for, and a few simple rules are followed (see Chapter 7).

Points to Watch

Trees, Shrubs and Climbers

Buy in autumn or spring. Although container-grown shrubs and trees can be planted at any time of the year – apart from the height of summer or the depths of winter – the traditional planting times of autumn and spring are still the best.

Check the name. To be sure of getting what you want it is worth paying the extra for 'named varieties'.

Check hardiness and that the tree or shrub is suitable for your site and the depth and type of your soil. It is a good idea to make a list of trees which appeal and are suitable for the planned sculpture, and to eliminate those which are unlikely to tolerate the prevailing growing conditions. You can then make an informed choice.

Calculate the ultimate space needed for the sculpture, and its proximity to buildings, drains and other services. No tree should be planted closer to a building than a distance equal to its ultimate height.

Go for container-grown plants every time in order to give your sculpture the best possible start, as the root disturbance and setback is minimal at planting. Avoid any plants which are wilting or have dried out, with compost shrinking away from the sides of the container. Avoid any which are badly pot-bound, are too big for their container, or have rooted into the ground. Steer clear of any which show signs of movement and flop about – you will be much better off with well-rooted plants which are firmly anchored in their containers.

Opt for trees and shrubs with a well-balanced framework of branches. Lopsided trees are not worth the risk you take of being able to prune them to shape afterwards – they are rarely successful. The main stem should be straight and strong and of a thickness that is in proportion to its height. Avoid standards and pyramids with a narrow crotch – they are more likely to snap off than those which branch away with a wide angle from the main stem. Remember also that the biggest plants in a batch are not necessarily the best.

Always look for plants which are free of pests, disease and other suspicious signs of ailments.

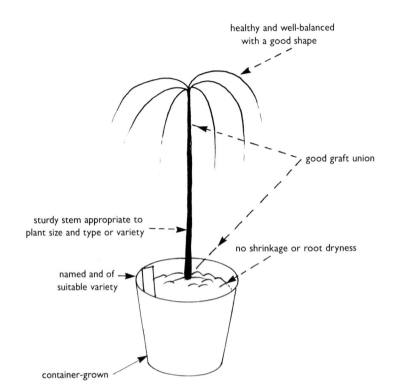

healthy and well-balanced
with a good shape

good graft union

sturdy stem appropriate to
plant size and type or variety

no shrinkage or root dryness

named and of
suitable variety

container-grown

Points to watch when buying trained plants.

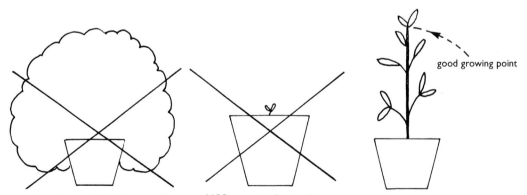

good growing point

not pot-bound or too big for its container   NOR overpotted in too big a pot

Points to watch when buying young plants to train.

Look for healthy foliage of good colour which is free from blemish. With evergreens, avoid any which have obviously lost some of their foliage – this is vital with conifers, as bare stems rarely break away again. Leave well alone any trees and shrubs which have quite obviously been hanging around in the nursery for some time.

With grafted trees, you should avoid any which show signs of large and unsightly graft unions.

Herbaceous Perennials

Buy in spring.

Avoid plants being sold from draughty shop fronts and outdoor displays. Plants must be well hardened off.

For training as standards and pyramids, plants must be unstopped, unless they are already of the right height (see Chapter 6).

Avoid plants with hard growth, as well as those which are lanky.

PLANTS' SUITABILITY FOR TRAINING

Topiary Sculptures	
Traditional topiary work	Buy ordinary nursery stock pyramids
Clipped hedge work	As above, or buy untrained, strong-growing, young nursery stock
Knot gardens and parterres	Buy untrained young stock
Treillage	Buy good container-grown plants, preferably trained up supports
Pleaching	Buy ordinary nursery stock standards
Pinch and prune sculptures	
Weeping standards Traditional standards Pyramids Fans Espaliers Cordons	Buy ordinary nursery stock. Where there is time in hand, substantial savings can be made by opting for lining out/growing on stock in the case of fans, espaliers and cordons.
Bonsai and container-grown miniatures	Buy young, untrained container-grown specimens
Carpet bedding sculptures	Buy hardened-off, well-rooted, pot-grown plants.
Half-hardy herbaceous sculptures	
(to be grown as standards and pyramids)	Buy as part-trained standards and pyramids. Alternatively, go for unstopped young plants.

Avoid overpotted plants – succulents in particular are prone to souring and rotting.

For carpet bedding an even-sized batch is ideal.

Transporting Plants Home

Don't carry your trees and shrubs home unprotected in an open car boot or on a roof rack, as irreparable damage can be done this way. If they won't go inside the vehicle, wrap them up well in fine mesh netting or hessian before starting out. Similarly, don't allow perennials which have not been hardened off to get chilled.

PREPARING FOR PLANTING

Once planting positions have been decided, you can push ahead with preparatory work, and planting can then start as soon as ground conditions allow. Container-grown trees, shrubs and climbers are best set out in autumn or spring, and half-hardy perennials should be planted out in late May/early June (or as soon as all danger of frost has past).

It is assumed that new gardens have been cleared of builders' rubble and topsoiled with levelling, and that someone has attended to the drainage. Similarly, in existing gardens overcrowded trees and shrubs will have been pruned back to let in light and air to make way for new stock. This is a good time to sort out poor drainage, and this is best approached from several angles. First, you can deal with the subsoil by constructing rubble-filled soakaways. At the lowest point of the problem area, excavate a hole 2½ft (75cm) square and 3ft (1m) deep. Fill to within 12in (30cm) of the top with clean rubble, levelling and consolidating after each 6in (15cm) layer has been added. (If you fail to firm it at this stage, you risk subsidence later on.) Spread a 2in (5cm) layer of clean gravel before finally levelling the whole off with the topsoil, which should have been kept to one side when you were digging the hole. You can expect a soakaway of this size to drain an area of 25sq yds (20sq m).

Next, you should aim to divert water running off adjacent higher land and hard-surfaced areas. Dig out a system of trenches, positioning them so that they trap the run-off

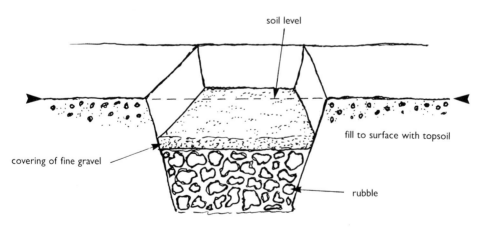

Making a rubble soakaway or sump.

soil level

fill to surface with topsoil

covering of fine gravel

rubble

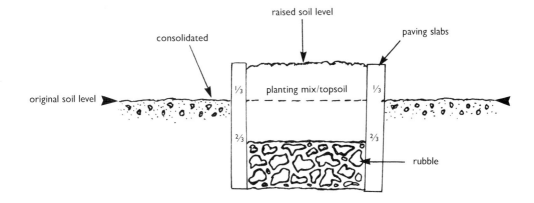

consolidated

raised soil level

paving slabs

original soil level

⅓

planting mix/topsoil

⅓

⅔

⅔

rubble

Making a raised bed.

water, and making them 12in (30cm) deep and of a similar width. Fill with rubble, topped off with gravel, and run them to a rubble soakaway set at a lower level. Such trenches also make it possible to grow a topiary hedge on what would otherwise be unsuitable low-lying wet ground. In this case you should make the trench parallel to the hedge and about 2ft (60cm) out from it. Finally, you can improve water percolation through the soil by good cultivations (see soil preparations, page 19).

Raised Beds

In heavy rainfall areas, growing plant sculptures in raised beds or containers often proves to be the best answer to poor natural drainage. This is also the case when ground conditions are otherwise unsatisfactory – the soil is shallow and poor; a thin layer of good topsoil overlies impenetrable rock; existing soils are infertile due to excess alkalinity, salinity or pollution; the subsoil is chalk and a lime-hater is the chosen tree or shrub; or sculptures are to be grown on a hard-surfaced area.

A useful bed size for a single specimen is 2 × 2ft (60 × 60cm), increasing to 4 ×3ft

(1.2 × 1m) for a small multiple feature. Brick, stone and concrete are the most durable construction materials, and the minumum thickness should be 4½in (1 1cm). Build on a 4in (10cm) thick and 8in (20cm) wide concrete foundation. Calculate on a 12ft (3.6m) tree sculpture needing a minimum 2ft (60cm) of good topsoil, and, to minimise summer watering, no more than two-thirds of this should be above the surrounding ground.

Replanting

Extra care is called for when you are planting on land that has been recently cleared of other trees and shrubs – there is always the risk of carrying over pests and disease.

Get rid of stumps after felling. You can ease out small stumps by digging round the base and manhandling, but with large stumps it is probably better to consider hiring a chipper, complete with operator, which decimates by flails. Failing this, saw the stump off close to the ground and treat it with a powerful chemical. Drill ½in (1cm) diameter holes into butt and top of the stump – make them 2in (5cm) deep, a similar distance apart and as near to vertical as possible. Part-fill them with potassium nitrate, and then plug them to prevent the rain washing away the chemical. Examine regularly and top up as necessary. It will take a stump anything from 2 to 10 years to rot away completely.

If you are replanting after the removal of a diseased tree or shrub it is vital to disinfect the soil first. Take away all obviously infected soil before forking up and drenching with proprietary soil disinfectant, following the manufacturer's recommendations. Deal with infected tools at the same time. Always wear protective clothing if this is specified, and delay planting until all fumes have dispersed.

Polluted Soil

In towns the long-term build-up of soot and grime often makes soils infertile. Liming and manuring can help, but in the case of pollution from seepage and spillage you should dig out affected soil and replace with fresh, after taking steps to avoid further pollution.

Liming and pH

You can correct soil acidity by applying ground limestone at the rate indicated by a soil test (*see* page 18). Correcting very alkaline soils is difficult, and the easiest solution is either to choose plants that are alkaline lovers, or to grow your trees or shrubs in raised beds or containers.

Beds and Planting Strips

Whether you are preparing beds for knot gardens, parterres or for growing on nursery stock, or whether you are getting planting strips ready for hedge topiaries, the cultivation procedures are much the same. Double digging is recommended – picking out perennial weeds and large stones, and forking

in generous amounts of well-rotted compost, manure or peat. If the land is weedy, clean it up. It is pointless planting on dirty ground and expecting plant sculptures to succeed. The best way to treat dirty land is to leave it vacant during the summer, as this allows for persistent hoeing, forking or rotavating which will weaken and kill most weeds. For those who wish to resort to chemicals, the majority are most effective if they are applied during spring and early summer – the best thing is to follow the makers' instructions.

Just before planting, topdress with 1in (3cm) of peat, plus general fertiliser and bonemeal, at the rate of 2oz of each per sq yd (70g per sq m). Cultivate it all into the top 4in (10cm) of soil.

Where the soil is very dry, gently apply about 2 gallons of water per sq yd (10 litres per sq m), some 24 hours before planting.

Planting Pockets

Always plant all but the smallest trees and shrubs into planting pockets. This applies to both wall-trained and free-standing ones.

For ordinary nursery stock, dig out holes at least 2ft (60cm) square and 1½ft (45cm) deep. Loosen up the sides and bottom, and fork in a bucketful of well-rotted garden compost, manure or peat, plus a handful of bonemeal. On heavy soil it is a good idea to work in a bucket of coarse sand at the same time.

Be ever-mindful of the fact that no free-standing tree should be planted closer to a building than a distance equal to its ultimate height, otherwise you risk damage to the foundations. Nor should any wall-trained tree be planted closer to a wall than 12in (30cm) – this would cause problems of stability and dryness. To restrict tree roots in order to prevent damage to foundations, services and drains, you should grow the plants in containers. Alternatively, you could construct

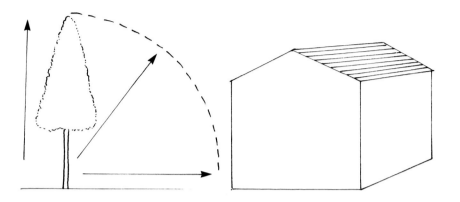

Ideal planting distance from a building for a direct-planted tree should equal the tree's *ultimate* height.

a tree box. To do this, you excavate a hole 3ft (90cm) square, and of a similar depth, at a point where there is no danger of interfering with undergound services. Line it with 4½in (11cm) of concrete, and put 12in (30cm) of consolidated rubble in the bottom before part-filling it with planting mix.

Planting Mix

To get plant sculptures off to a good start you must use a good planting mix. Standard soil-based composts are popular for the purpose, but you will need to opt for peat-based composts if your trees or shrubs have been raised in these. Fertilised and fortified planting mixes based on organic peat or bark soil conditioners can be tricky to handle. Home-made mixes come into their own where the existing topsoil is reasonable — weed, pest and disease free — and only needs fortifying. In this case, mix together two 2-gallon (9-litre) buckets of finely-sieved topsoil; half a bucket each of peat and coarse sand; and ½lb (225g) of general fertiliser. Add 1 part peat to 3 parts of mix if it is to be used for planting trees raised in peat-based mixes.

(For details of specialist supports *see* Chapter 5 for topiary, Chapter 6 for pinch and prune, and Chapter 2 for containers.)

Single Vertical Stake

Drive your stake in after the planting hole has been dug out but *before* the tree is lowered into position — this reduces the risk of root injury. Set the stake slightly off-centre and into the direction of the prevailing wind. The tree is then blown away from the stake rather than towards it, which would bring about the risk of chafing. Visually it is better to position the stake behind the trunk (looking from the main viewing point), but only do this in a sheltered garden. About 18in (45cm) of the stake should be sunk below ground, and with standards the top should be 2in (5cm) below the bottom branch. Secure trees to stakes with two ties — one at the top and the other about half-way down — and use proprietary ties with spacers. Never be tempted to tie in plants with wire — it cuts into stems and can kill.

25

SUPPORTS

With plant sculptures the initial supports can be critical.

Supports	Uses
Cane/tubular metal stake	Young pyramids and standards Young growing-on stock
Single vertical stake	Weeping and traditional standards and pyramids – ordinary nursery stock
Single vertical stake with wire rose frame	All climbers and weeping standards
Arches	Treillage and clipped topiary features
Pergolas	Treillage
Tripods and pillars	Climbers and trailers
Pre-shaped wire frames	Topiaries and treillage, carpet bedding
Trellis (free-standing and wall-mounted)	Treillage, pinch and prune espaliers and fans, and wall topiary
Rustic screens	Treillage, pinch and prune espaliers and fans
Post and wire (wall-mounted and free-standing	Treillage, pinch and prune cordon, espalier and fan, and wall topiary

rose trainer or stake for weeping standards

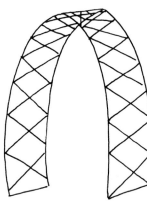

wire, metal or timber arch frame

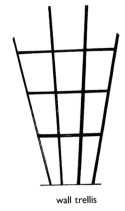

wall trellis

Supports for plant sculptures.

Wall-mounted Wires

Use 14-gauge taut horizontal wires fixed to the wall with threaded vine eyes, which are screwed into previously drilled and plugged holes. Set the vine eyes no more than 4ft (1.2m) apart, and secure the bottom wire about 12in (30cm) above ground, with succeeding wires a similar distance apart, one above the other. With cordon and fan-trained forms attach bamboo canes to the wires, and tie branches in to these at 6–12in (15–30cm) intervals. With espaliers, adjust the spacings to suit the branch arrangements. When training against a fence you can simply attach the wires to the fence posts, provided they are no wider apart than 6ft (1.8m).

Wall-mounted Trellis

Leave an air space of 1in (3cm) between trellis and wall.

Free-standing Post and Wire Sculptures

Space posts no more than 7ft (2m) apart and arrange wires to suit.

PLANTING

Preparing Plants

Harden off *all* indoor-raised plants thoroughly before setting out. Water all container plants an hour or two before planting and allow them to drain thoroughly before disturbing them again.

Pocket Planting Container Trees

Remove the trees from their containers. Cut floppy containers open and peel back, taking care not to damage young roots. Knock plants out of rigid pots – this should not be difficult if the compost is moist. Gently tease out the roots encircling the rootball, without breaking up the ball of soil – roots left tangled at planting time rarely grow into the surrounding soil. Trim any roots which are damaged, and position the plants in their prepared holes. (If you are planting trees, tie them loosely to their stake to steady them.) Work planting mix around the rootball, firming well – resist the temptation to joggle the plant – and, finally, level off with the surrounding soil.

When you are planting wall-trained sculptures it is worth installing some form of deep watering system. Two 12in (30cm) lengths of drain-pipe, set one on each side of the rootball, with the tops slightly exposed, works well. Packed around with planting mix, the pipes are filled with stones or gravel, and water poured in at the top will soak down to the roots.

Row Planting

This is for hedge sculptures, knot gardens and parterres. Plant direct into well-prepared beds. With hedge topiaries, plant on a slight ridge if the soil is inclined to be wet and heavy. Thereafter, mulch to prevent soil wash, and, should there be any evidence of this, build the soil back up immediately. On dry, sandy soils, plant in a shallow trench, to prevent surface water run-off.

Massed Carpet Bedding

Where wire frames are not used, plant direct into well-prepared beds. You should work from planks on the soil, and from the centre of the bed outwards.

27

POST PLANTING CARE

You must protect newly set-out, autumn-planted, frost-sensitive trees such as magnolia. A 6in (15cm) layer of straw, held in place with pegged-down netting will suffice.

Shelter *all* autumn-planted trees and shrubs from cold and drying winds in exposed gardens. This is especially vital with evergreens. You should protect them on three sides with fine mesh netting supported on a light framework. Shelter rows or groups of plants by erecting wind screens of fine mesh netting or permeable fencing across the path of the prevailing wind. Net wall-trained sculptures against bud-stripping birds, and, where rabbits are likely to be a problem, use proprietary tree guards.

As soon as soil conditions allow, refirm trees and shrubs lifted by frost or wind, and soil over any exposed roots.

During their first spring and summer you must keep all newly-planted trees and shrubs well watered. In dry weather you ought to be thinking in terms of 4 gallons (20 litres) per watering. Watering in dribbles encourages shallow rooting. Where deep watering systems are installed, water up to two or three times a day in dry weather when you are trying to get trees established. In low rainfall areas and on sandy soil it helps to scoop up loose soil to form a ridge, about 2ft (60cm) out from the trunk, so that the tree stands in a shallow 'dish'. This has the desired effect of reducing surface water run-off, but you must be careful not to expose any roots. After hot, dry, windy days hose down the foliage. This is most important with evergreens.

Lightly hoe over the root run to break the soil crust in spring. Remove weeds, water and apply a surface mulch of well-rotted garden compost, manure or peat. If supplies are limited, consider using black plastic perforated sheet. If this is camouflaged under a layer of gravel it doesn't look *too* bad.

After planting out half-hardy perennials keep them well watered, and staked where appropriate.

Keep an eye on all stakes and ties and adjust as necessary.

2 Growing in Containers

USING CONTAINERS

Advantages

Containers overcome any problems the gardener might encounter with unsuitable soil, and they also make it possible to grow plant sculptures on hard-surfaced areas. They thus provide a measure of flexibility, at the same time giving extra height and prominence to displays. Since containerising restricts development and keeps roots out of harm's way, it is the obvious way (and often the only way) to deal with tree and shrub sculptures in small gardens.

Implications

There is an increased dependence of plants when they are grown in containers and without regular attention to watering, feeding and repotting success will be remote. Timely attention throughout the year is essential – for instance, tree and shrub sculptures will need extra protection from frost, wind and heavy rain.

When you are planting in containers it is just as important to match the needs of the plants with the environment as it is when planting direct. You must consider the effects of the sun and shade; shelter and exposure to wind; and suitability of containers and composts.

Standing Areas

All containerised plant sculptures must be ensured of free drainage at the base. Stand containers on a gravel bed so that the water will seep away. Water-tight drip trays should only be used in summer, or when the containers are raised up on legs. Don't make the common mistake of putting these trays under permanent tree and shrub sculptures – you will risk waterlogging in winter.

Winter Quarters

Hardy Bonsai and miniature plant sculptures need to stand under frames or purpose-built Bonsai shelters for the duration of the winter. Half-hardy shrub and tree sculptures, along with herbaceous perennial standards and the like, need the winter protection of a frost-free greenhouse or plant room.

CHOOSING CONTAINERS

Size

For an average shrub sculpture you should look for a container with a minimum depth and diameter of 12in (30cm). A 10ft (3m) high tree sculpture will ultimately need a 24in (60cm) container to hold sufficient compost for sustenance and anchorage. It is normal to grow Bonsai in shallow dishes, but miniature tree sculptures will need a container of about 5in (12cm).

Drainage

Containers must have plenty of drainage holes in the base, especially those exposed to rain.

There should be no fewer than three 1in (3cm) holes to a 15in (38cm) container.

Stability and Shape

Avoid top-heavy containers, as they are likely to topple. Be wary of fibreglass, plastic and wood fibre containers – they rely on the sheer weight of the compost for stability, and at the smaller end of the range they can blow over all too easily. For ease of potting and watering the top of a container should be as wide as, or wider than, the rest of the container (Bonsai dishes excepted).

Durability

Frost resistance and good thermal qualities are characteristics of high priority for permanent outdoor sculptures, where roots are extremely vulnerable to extremes of heat and cold. The containers also need to last well. Hardwood, concrete and reconstituted stone are among the most practical materials – terracotta pots are likely to shatter in frost. Specialist hard-fired Bonsai dishes are the exception, since they stand up well to frost and wear. Metal, fibreglass, plastics and wood fibre containers are all poor insulators, but fibre liners can often help if there is no alternative.

Appearance

Steer clear of fussy design and bright colours – they will compete with the sculpture for attention.

COMPOSTS

Never use ordinary garden soil when you are growing plants in containers. It pans down badly and contains too little air; it usually drains too slowly and holds too much water; and there is always a risk of importing soil pests and diseases. Most proprietary potting composts avoid these shortcomings.

Soil-based composts are a balanced mixture of sterilised soil and peat, plus aggregate, fertiliser and limestone.

Peat-based composts are without soil, and the other ingredients are adjusted accordingly.

For average sculpture work soil-based composts are preferable, especially for long-stay plants such as trees and shrubs. Not only are they easier to manage but they also retain their physical qualities much longer than peat-based mixtures. Soil-based composts are also heavier, so containers are less likely to blow over. However, when you are potting up plants which have been raised in peat-based mixtures, you should continue to use these. Alternatively, use a mix of equal parts peat-based and soil-based compost to make the transition less of a shock for the plant. Subsequent potting could then be into a soil-based mixture.

It is sound practice to buy proprietary ready-to-use potting composts. On a small scale they usually work out cheaper and more convenient, and they are much more reliable than composts prepared at home. Until recently it was the norm to buy a weak compost for propagation and potting young plants, a standard compost for normal potting, and a strong mix for hungry vigorous-growing plants and top dressings. Today, many gardeners prefer to use general purpose composts, which are fine, provided fertiliser levels are boosted. Mix in a handful of bonemeal per bucketful of compost for general potting, and double this for mature trees and shrubs, vigorous growers and top dressings.

Special Compost Mixtures

Seek out lime-free composts for plants intolerant of lime (*see* plant guide).

Bonsai Composts

Most Bonsai will grow well in a mixture of two parts general purpose soil-based potting compost to one part each of sphagnum peat and coarse sand, plus a handful of bonemeal per bucketful of mix. As with any other trees, you must always heed lime requirements.

POTTING

When to Pot?

Never pot in winter when there is always the risk of a setback. Spring is one of the best times to deal with most container plants, especially in cold areas, and you should aim to pot deciduous kinds before their buds burst. (Bonsai should *always* be potted in spring.) Autumn is the other main potting time, and it is particularly good for deciduous trees and shrubs, and for vulnerable trees such as birch, Japanese maple and flowering crab, which are all prone to bleeding.

First Potting

Pot up seedlings and cuttings before they become tall and spindly.

General Potting

Pot on all growing-on stock as soon as the roots are seen to encircle the rootball – using pots two sizes up – until the ultimate-sized container is reached. You should then repot mature sculptures into a container of the same size as the preceding one.

Why Pot?

You must repot your plants to give them more space as they grow. The aim is to increase the rootball size so that it is in keeping with the top growth. Take note that when thick roots start to grow out of the bottom of the container the ideal time to pot has passed.

Repotting also tops up nutrients and provides larger reserves of food and water. Warning signs which call for prompt attention are small, pale, starved leaves and unthrifty plants. By repotting you are providing a fresh rooting medium. Don't delay potting if the potting shows any signs of rapid drying out, even after frequent watering.

Preparing Containers

Clean and disinfect all containers. Soak new porous terracotta and concrete ones for at least twenty-four hours in clean water – this will remove harmful alkali and rehydrate the container. When preparing containers to stand outdoors, cover the drainage holes with gauze or plastic mesh, otherwise compost loss can be excessive. There is also a strong likelihood of pests crawling up through the

gauze over drainage hole

Preparing containers for planting.

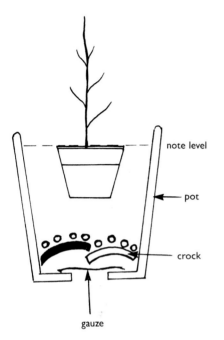

note level

pot

crock

gauze

Traditional potting.

drainage holes. Bottom out all containers with coarse gravel, crocks or small stones, to a depth of about an eighth of the container's height – this is for effective drainage. When preparing for long-term trees and shrubs, cover over the drainage aggregate with damp peat. Finally part-fill the container with moist potting compost – it will then be ready for planting.

Getting the Plants Ready

Soak all plants thoroughly and allow them to drain for at least an hour before disturbing them. Temporarily tie in any plant where it will make for ease of handling. Clip (see Chapter 5) and pinch and prune (see Chapter 6), and also take the opportunity to pick over and clean up the plants, cutting out dead wood in the case of trees and shrubs.

Finally, check for pests and diseases and take preventive measures (see Chapter 8).

Having removed the plant from its container, tease out any remaining crocks or gravel and gently untangle the roots, without breaking up the rootball. Set the plant in its prepared container and pack around with moist compost, leaving a space at the top for watering. (Be careful with peat-based mixtures – they should not be packed down too tightly.)

Points to Watch

Herbaceous Standards

To encourage plenty of healthy root growth, don't firm too hard. For straight stems and balanced heads, ensure plants are potted vertically and retied to their supports immediately. In order to maintain a clear stem, clean up any secondary growth branching away at the base – left unchecked, these growths will sap the plants of their strength. You should pot trained standards each spring.

Trees and Shrubs

Tease away and uncoil roots at the base, and shorten them slightly. If the rootball exceeds 10in (25cm), prune harder, taking width and depth down by about a quarter. Trim all damaged roots back to sound tissue. Lightly loosen up the sides of the rootball before positioning it in the new container – this should be 2in (5cm) wider than the original, or 3in (8cm) in the case of larger trees. Adjust the compost level so that the top of the rootball is set 1½in (4cm) below the level of the rim, with the plant central and upright. When infilling between the rootball and the side of the container, firm well as filling proceeds, then top up to within ¾in (2cm) of the rim.

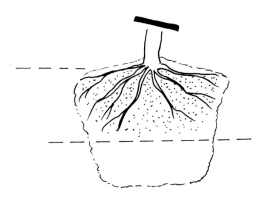

Root pruning – for Bonsai, reduce by one-quarter to one-third when potting from normal container into Bonsai dish.

Bonsai

When moving young trees from conventional pots to shallow Bonsai dishes, reduce rootball depth by up to a half – the crown should also be thinned to compensate for root loss. Choose a container with a diameter of not less than half tree height or spread so that the specimen looks 'comfortable'. Set the plant at the rim of the container, or very slightly above it, bearing in mind that most young trees need to be wired firmly into position to steady them. Work Bonsai compost around the roots and firm.

REPOTTING

Once tree, shrub and climber sculptures have reached the maximum size that is in keeping with their setting, the accepted practice is to repot them into the same-sized container. This keeps them healthy, without allowing them to get appreciably larger. Having removed the plant from its container, carefully tease out as much of the old compost as possible, using a pointed stick. Reduce rootball

size by cutting away the main roots from the lower quarter of the rootball and taking in the width. Repot without delay.

With Bonsai, tease out the old compost, trim the roots very lightly and wire back into place. Infill with Bonsai compost, and if possible top off with moss, wiring this into place if necessary with bent pins.

TOPDRESSING

Established Tree and Shrub Sculptures

You will find that it is not necessary to repot every year. Indeed, it is more normal to topdress in alternate years, or even in two years out of three. Remove weeds, and scrape away moss and old surface compost, taking care not to cause damage to the roots. Top up with fresh strong compost. If compost has already been washed away, leaving roots exposed, simply clean up the surface, prick to loosen the crust, and top up. Never dig out the compost or irreparable damage to roots is likely.

Bonsai

Topdress with fresh compost whenever the feeding roots are exposed– usually every 6 to 8 weeks.

General

As soon as compost has been washed away from any container-grown sculpture, you should topdress with fresh. This applies with trees, shrubs, climbers and herbaceous standards.

IMMEDIATE GENERAL AFTERCARE

Support

Stake and tie all tall and floppy plants, using split canes for young stock, canes or tubular grow sticks for standards and pyramids, and wire supports for more elaborate sculptures (*see* Chapter I).

Watering

Water thoroughly after potting and subsequently keep moist. Use a can with a fine rose to minimise wash-down of compost. Bonsai excepted – always water Bonsai from below by standing in a bucket of water of up to two-thirds their container depth.) Mist over newly-potted plants every day – this is especially important with Bonsai – and continue to do so until herbaceous plants are growing away freely and trees, shrubs and climbers are re-established. Thereafter, moisten during the evening after warm, dry or windy days.

Note Don't spray echeveria, sedum or sempervivum overhead – you will run the risk of them rotting.

Shade

Protect newly-potted plants from direct sun. With moveable containers the easiest way is to stand them in light shade until they are re-established. Alternatively, use lath or fine mesh netting screens. Bonsai are very vulnerable and *must* be shaded.

Wind

Wind is a hazard second only to dryness. Provide adequate shelter until the plants are re-established, and thereafter you must also provide protection in exposed gardens.

Heavy Rain

Shelter is necessary – *see* page 44.

SPECIALIST CONTAINERS

Carpet Bedding Features

Carpet bedding 3D characters are most frequently seen at major flower shows, and until recent cutbacks they were also relatively commonplace in public parks, and in open spaces at popular seaside resorts, particularly during illumination displays. Rarely are such novelties reproduced in private gardens, but there is no reason why they should not be. They always make a talking point. Making up these features is not too difficult. It is largely a case of adapting the principles involved in making up wire hanging baskets, with a little imagination and improvisation thrown in.

Containers

The requirements are modest – nothing more daunting than 1½in (4cm) mesh wire netting, tie wires, canes, plastic sheet or moss, plus potting compost and plants.

Method

It is best to start with a simple shape, before attempting anything too ambitious, and always work out a planting system or design on graph paper before you begin.

A **tortoise** is a suitable subject to start with. Using the wire mesh, fashion out the underpart of the body in the form of an oval dish, and position it where it is going to stand for the duration of the summer. Use pieces of cane for support and cross ties, but make sure they can be hidden from view after planting. Line the sides and bottom of the 'dish' with plastic sheet – or moss, if available – and part-fill with fresh, moist potting compost. Start planting round the sides, pushing the roots through the plastic and wire into the moist compost. If the rootball is too big to pass through the wire, simply snip the wire to make space rather than damage and reduce the roots. Continue to alternate planting with the addition of more compost until the sides of the 'dish' are completely covered with plants and the centre of the dish is filled with compost. At this stage you can form the foundation of the 'shell' by building up compost in a domed mound. Cover over with plastic or moss and overlay with a piece of loose mesh netting, cut to size. Plant the 'shell' through the netting, starting at one end and

working systematically to the other. Finally, tie in the wire of the 'shell' and secure it to the underpart of the body. The head and legs are made of plastic- or moss-lined, compost-filled, mesh netting cylinders, of a size in proportion to the body. Once they are in position they are planted and the ends are sealed.

A **snail** complete with shell is quite feasible too. Make a sausage-shaped body with a 'head' and 'tail stub', and plant it up. Two knitting needles pushed into the head make realistic feelers. For the shell, fashion a circular cushion and superimpose it on to the body, holding it in place with canes.

You could also try an **owl** – an oval egg shape with a ball on top – or a **butterfly** – a central cylindrical tube tapering towards the

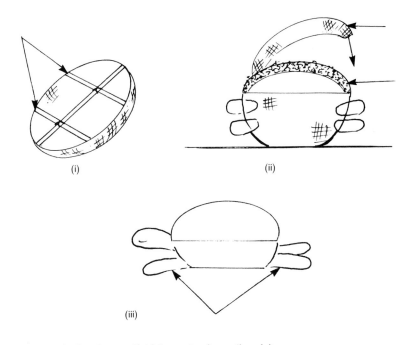

(i)

(ii)

(iii)

Making a tortoise carpet bed sculpture. (i) Make a wire frame 'boat', line with plastic sheet, and use canes for support and cross pieces to hold frame. (ii) Fill with potting compost to domed effect and cover with moss held in place with netting. Plant through sides and top. (iii) Use moss-lined, compost-filled wire mesh tubes for head and legs.

tail end, with a wing on either side.

Other fairly straightforward ideas are **decorative boxes, cubes, pyramids** or **cushions**. Make the shape which appeals to you with wire as before, and then strengthen it with concealed canes. Starting at the bottom, alternate filling and planting. A monogram could be worked on one side with plants such as echeveria, sedum or sempervivum.

When you want to move on to more tricky projects, you could consider teddy bears, elephants, horses and carpet bedding housing.

A Pin-Cushion Ball

Again, this is something a little out of the ordinary, which is inexpensive and very easy to execute. Use two 10in (25cm) plastic- or moss-lined wire-framed hanging baskets. Fill them with lightweight peat-based potting compost. Then comes the tricky bit – fixing the two filled baskets together without losing the compost. To do this, place a smooth, rigid plastic sheet over one of the baskets. Invert the basket holding the sheet firmly in position, and place it over the second basket. Carefully

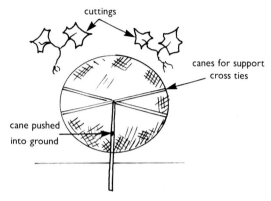

cuttings

canes for support
cross ties

cane pushed
into ground

To make a pin-cushion ball, fill wire mesh ball with compost and insert rooted ivy cuttings through the sides.

slide out the sheet and then wire the two baskets together.

Rooted cuttings of easy plants such as ivies are dibbled in thickly to cover sides, top and bottom completely. Once the plants are growing away nicely, you can suspend the globes in the same way as you would hanging baskets, or you can simply impale them on top of short stakes for display.

3 Routine Care

If plant sculptures are to flourish, there are certain routine jobs which must be tackled – in the correct manner and at the right time – in order to maintain good growing conditions. (For details of immediate aftercare *see* Chapters 1 and 2.)

WATERING

Incorrect watering is one of the most common causes of plant ailments. Too much results in suffocation and drowning of plant roots, while too little leads to wilting and the inability of the plant to function properly. Both extremes invariably bring about the demise of the plant.

Water Quality

Mains tap water is suitable for most plants, but in hard water districts, where the mains supply is rich in lime, it is important to collect and use rainwater for acid-loving plants such as rhododendrons, heather, magnolias and Bonsai. Never use water treated with chemical water softeners – given prolonged use they are harmful to plants.

Watering Methods

Direct-Planted Sculptures

Ball watering Water recently-planted trees, shrubs, climbers and half-hardy standards by drenching the rootball, preferably using a watering-can with a coarse rose. Rake any mulch to one side beforehand, replacing it immediately afterwards. For those who wish to water with a hose-pipe, you will need to be careful of your timing, otherwise serious over- or under-application is likely. You can easily work out the flow rate per minute by filling a bucket of known size with water and calculating accordingly.

If surface water run-off is a problem when ball watering, make a shallow ridge of soil around each plant to trap the water. Be sure to remember to break down the ridges before the autumn rains.

Sprinkler watering Direct-planted carpet bedding parterres and knot garden plots are more easily watered with sprinklers. The danger is that you may not leave the sprinkler on long enough for the water to get down to the roots – check with a trowel. In hot, dry weather you should water once or twice a week during the evening, or in dull weather, but never in strong sun. Don't ever use sprinklers where sedums, echeveria or sempervivum are involved – you will risk rotting the plants. In such cases it is far better to water between plants with a long-spouted can.

Deep watering Where provision has been made for deep watering (*see* Chapter 1), water as normal down the drain-pipes, and then apply a third extra again as a surface drench.

Deep watering – pour water down drain-pipes (set in soil when planting and angled towards the root ball).

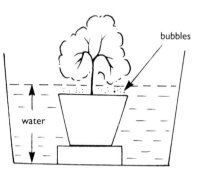

Plunge watering. Place dried-out plants in a container of water filled to a level just above pot. Remove and drain when bubbles stop rising – about 20 minutes.

Container Sculptures

Traditional method Pour water gently into the top of the container and continue until it dribbles out at the bottom.

Watering from below This is the method used for Bonsai and miniature sculptures. Stand containers to half their depth in water and leave until the surface is visibly moist, then drain.

Plunge watering Use this method as a last resort when plants have dried out and the rootball has shrunk back from the container sides. Container and rootball are submerged and left until the bubbles cease to rise. After allowing the plant to drain, repot. If the dried-out container is immovable, infill by packing moist compost into the space down the sides, using a pointed stick. Then hose on water for 10 minutes or so, with the tap turned on low and a small pot placed over the end of the hose.

When and How Much

The amount of water to apply must be varied according to the prevailing conditions, soil type, kind of plant and the time of year.

Trees, shrubs and climbers, recently set out in the ground, need watering during hot, dry spells in spring and summer for the first year or two after planting. Thereafter they can usually fend for themselves. About 2 gallons (10 litres) per plant every three or four days is a good average watering. Thorough soaking encourages deep rooting, and the deeper the roots, the better able the plants are to withstand subsequent dry weather. Step up watering to daily during periods of prolonged drought on quick-draining, light, sandy soils.

During hot, dry, drought-stricken conditions, larger tree and shrub sculptures should be given about 4 gallons (20 litres) per sq yd (sq m) over the entire root run. This equates with 1in (3cm) of rainfall. If the soil surface is compacted, spike systematically over the root area with a fork prior to watering. This will assist percolation, but you must take care not to damage the roots.

Container-grown trees, shrubs, climbers and half-hardy perennials all need frequent watering in spring and summer, but must be watered sparingly in winter. You should allow the compost to nearly dry out between waterings – in summer this usually entails daily watering, or twice daily during very hot weather. If in doubt about when to water, newcomers should use a moisture meter. Once experience is gained, the need to water becomes instinctive.

Hosing Down

Hose clean water over the foliage of new tree and shrub sculptures in the evening during warm, dry weather, and whenever they have received a buffeting from drying winds. Similarly, in towns, hose down evergreens occasionally to remove soot and grime. In hard water areas, use rainwater instead of mains supply for acid lovers, Bonsai and miniatures.

FEEDING

Growing plants need a steady supply of nutrients, and losses must be made good if plants are to flourish.

What to Use

Choose a complete proprietary fertiliser in preference to making up mixtures at home – they involve less work, are more reliable and no more costly. Those with an analysis of 7 per cent of nitrogen, phosphorus and potassium are excellent for general use. Look for brands with added trace elements.

Dry Fertilisers or Liquid Feeds?

Dry fertilisers, especially the granular formulations, are longer lasting than liquid feeds, so need fewer applications. However, they also act more slowly. As a general guide, you should use dry fertilisers for topdressing trees, shrubs and climbers planted out permanently in beds and borders, while container plants, and short-stay plants set out in beds, will respond best to regular liquid feeding. Liquid feeds are useful where a nutritional deficiency is suspected, and they can also serve to provide a quick boost during the growing season. This might perhaps be needed where young trees and shrubs were set out on poor or sandy soils and have not had time to develop a vigorous root system, or where tree and shrub sculptures appear starved in areas of high rainfall.

Foliar feeding (whereby extremely dilute, quick-acting liquid feeds are sprayed directly on to leaves) has its uses too, particularly for reviving plants which are under stress. You must always foliar feed on a dull day, otherwise you risk scorching the plants. Apply evenly, thoroughly wetting the leaves, and only use proprietary feeds that have been specially formulated for the purpose, following the makers' directions carefully. Reserve foliar feeds for smooth and shiny-leaved trees, shrubs and hardy plants. It is not suitable for hairy, delicate or fleshy-leaved subjects, such as the majority of those used in carpet bedding features.

When to Feed

Before feeding, always make sure the soil or compost is moist. During dry weather, water thoroughly the day prior to feeding – think in terms of applying 4 gallons (20 litres) of water per sq yd (sq m) over the entire root run.

Direct-planted Subjects

As a general rule, you should not root feed newly-planted trees for the first two years, nor shrubs and climbers during their first year, apart from those which are growing on sandy and impoverished soils. Make the roots work. Thereafter, give a light dressing in the early spring of general fertiliser, at the rate of a small

39

handful per sq yd (sq m) spread over the root run prior to mulching. Hoe the feed into the top Iin (3cm) or so of soil. Surface-rooting magnolias, camellias, rhododendrons and conifers cannot be treated in the same way. For them, you should sprinkle the feed over the soil, and water it in – don't hoe or you will risk root damage. If the roots are exposed, mix the dry fertiliser with double the quantity of loose topsoil before spreading it – this will avoid root scorch. It would be ideal in these circumstances to topdress with Iin (3cm) minimum layer of soil-based potting compost.

Where the soil is poor or sandy, increase the above fertiliser rates by up to half as much again, and similarly where the sculpture is growing in grass. With these heavier applications it is, however, better to split them into two, and apply the fertiliser at 14-day intervals. Another alternative to stepping up the dry feed is to boost with liquid feeds during the summer months.

Keep a close watch on magnolias, Japanese maples, heathers, camellias, rhododendrons, crab apple, roses and wisteria, especially if the garden overlies chalk or limestone and the topsoil layer is thin. If they become unthrifty, you should act as if you suspect chlorosis and soil drench with iron sequestrene.

Container Sculptures

The rules for liquid feeding for plants in containers are the same as for watering – carry on until it trickles out at the base.

About three weeks after potting or top-dressing give all freely-growing plants a balanced high potash tomato-type liquid feed, and repeat at fortnightly to three-weekly intervals for trees and shrubs (make it every week to ten days for herbaceous standards). Give Bonsai feed that you have made up at half the recommended strength. This not only avoids excessive growth but also minimises the risk of root scorching given their extremely confined root run.

Continue liquid feeding up to the end of August in mild areas, but stop early in the month in cold districts. If you feed any later there is a risk of plants making soft, sappy tip growth which will be liable to frost injury and dieback. The aim should always be to have well-ripened wood for topiary and all woody-stemmed sculptures. This is vital is cold exposed gardens. Similarly, soft sappy herbaceous plants are less likely to overwinter successfully than those with firm, ripe growth.

MULCHING

Spring Mulching

This is very important, especially for recently-planted or pleached hedge topiaries as well as pinch and prune single specimen features. Unfortunately, it is an activity which is all too often neglected. A good mulch will keep roots cool during summer, conserve valuable moisture and smother seedling weeds. It will also prevent the formation of a surface crust. This enables rain or irrigation water to percolate, so discouraging the erosion of the topsoil by surface run-off. Over the years, mulching with peat, garden compost or manure will gradually increase the depth of good topsoil, and in turn this will ensure good growth of topiary, and hardy woody-stemmed sculptures in particular.

Once the weather has warmed up a little in the spring, apply a generous surface mulch to hardy trees, shrubs and climbers, using peat, well-rotted garden compost, manure or shredded bark. In the case of shortages, give priority to newly set-out plants and consider using black plastic (see Chapter I). Hoe off surface weeds, water, topdress with fertiliser, then fork on the mulch. Keep an eye on the mulches during the growing season and try to keep them topped up, maintaining a 2–3in (5–8cm) layer.

In autumn, lightly fork in the remains of peat, compost and manure mulches. Replenish the bark – this should be left in place all year round. Top up the gravel cover over the black plastic sheeting. Incidently, plastic mulching sheeting needs to be lifted in the autumn of every second year, and then replaced the following spring.

Lightly cultivate the soil around the trees and shrubs which have not been mulched. This helps to conserve moisture by breaking up the crust – in effect forming a dust mulch.

Where supplies of mulch are plentiful, half-hardy standards and pyramids of such plants as fuchsias and geraniums also benefit greatly from mulching.

Winter Mulching

Mulch in October to protect the roots of recently-planted, frost-tender young trees and shrubs such as magnolia, camellia, griselinia, myrtus, olearia and piptanthus.

OTHER CARE

Ground Cultivations

Maintain a minimum 12in (30cm) collar of weed-free soil around the trunks of all trees and shrubs growing in grass – this is necessary for mulching. Also, if they are unchecked, grass and weeds will compete with the tree for food and moisture, and can also be held responsible for trunk rotting and defoliation of the lower branches. They will provide a breeding ground, too, for pests, particularly in the case of hedge topiaries. On all these counts, therefore, it is essential to keep the base of hedge topiaries free from weeds and

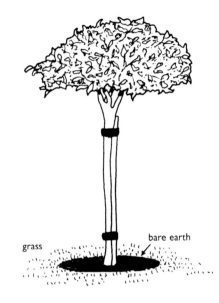

Earth collar around a newly-planted tree.

rubbish. (You should also think of the fire hazard in hot, dry weather – fire can undo years of topiary training and growth in minutes.) In the case of wall shrubs and climbers which are hemmed in by grass, you must allow a minimum 18in (45cm) semi-circular collar of bare earth for mulching. Wall plants are particularly prone to root dryness, and they must be mulched.

Check recently-planted trees, shrubs and climbers regularly, and refirm those which may be showing any signs of lift. Spread fresh soil or potting compost over exposed roots and firm again. In windswept gardens, it is a good idea to earth up around the plants in the autumn, at least for the first few years.

On heavy soils relieve surface compaction and panning by shallow forking in the autumn and again in the spring. This improves aeration and subsequent growth. Take care never to work heavy soils when wet, and if the ground is in any way soft and moist, always work from planks during maintenance operations to minimise compaction.

Pruning

Cut off **dead heads** promptly. Don't allow trees and shrubs to carry berries or fruits during the first season after planting. If a really severe winter follows autumn planting, you should remove flower buds before they open in an effort to conserve energy.

Remove **suckers** as soon as you see them – these are unwanted growths at or below soil level which, if left, will weaken the tree. They are best cut back to the point of origin. Similarly, you should cut out reverted green shoots on variegated plants.

Cut out **dead**, badly **diseased** or seriously **pest-infested** branches and shoots as and when necessary, regardless of the time of year. Also, shorten back straggly, untidy or misplaced growth as a matter of routine at the normal pruning time (see Part 2 for individual plant details).

Following a hard winter, **frost-scorched** and **browned** shoot tips and foliage should be removed – the best time will be late spring for most deciduous plants and broad-leaved evergreens. With conifers you should hold back the work until early summer. Don't be too hasty to remove large chunks of seemingly dead topiary or plant sculptures – wait until there is no shadow of doubt that the wood is dead. Always try the thumbnail test first – scrape away a bit of bark, and if there are signs of green underneath there is hope of life.

Doctor up **damaged** or **diseased bark** by cutting out and paring over with a sharp knife. Paint over wounds promptly with a suitable sealant.

Supporting and Tying

Check supports and ties at least once each season, and always immediately after exceptionally severe storms. Slacken off those which are too tight and likely to cut into the bark. Since slippage causes chafing and play increases the risk of snapping, take up any slack. Take note if ties have slipped down, as this always makes snapping off more likely. Check stakes for movement and look for signs of rotting at soil level. Once standard trees are well established, with firm roots, stakes can often be removed altogether.

Aim to tie in and train all new shoots during the growing season, before they get too long and damaged. If it isn't feasible to do the job properly, then tie them in loosely and temporarily until time permits. Certainly you should get them tied in permanently and made safe and secure before the onset of winter storms and snowfalls. Wall plants and climbers are perhaps most at risk.

PLANT PROTECTION

Frost

You should not allow frozen evergreen sculptures of any sort to thaw out too quickly – shade them until the process is over. Those in east-facing borders are most at risk, and irreparable damage can be done by too rapid a thaw in early morning sun. Knock heavy snowfalls off evergreen sculptures and shelter Bonsai and miniature sculptures from snow under cover (see below).

Direct-Planted Trees and Shrubs

Protect frost-sensitive roots with a generous layer of pegged-down straw (see plant guide for details on individual plants).

Container Sculptures

Move small container trees and shrubs into sheltered positions such as near to a warm house wall. Alternatively, they can go under cover, provided they can be given plenty of ventilation. Those near house walls need special watching (*see* page 44 on rain protection). Often the easiest way with a number of small containers is to plunge them into a bed of straw or leaves. Never leave container plants standing on raised display staging — their roots will be highly vulnerable to frost injury.

Bonsai and miniature plant sculptures overwintering under a frame or purpose-built shelter should be given added protection during severe frost. Throw fine mesh netting or old carpet over the frame at night. Leave the cover on in the morning to prevent too rapid a thaw but do remember to remove it during the course of the day. Treat young growing-on stock in a similar manner.

In spring harden off Bonsai which have been overwintered under frames, and be sure to give overhead protection from hail storms and frost right up to the end of May. The newly-opening young leaves are particularly sensitive to frost, wind and hail injury.

Large container trees and shrubs overwintering outdoors must have their roots well protected. Insulate the container with a minimum 6in (15cm) layer of straw or leaves, held in place with pinned-down netting. Cover the sides as well as the top of the rootball.

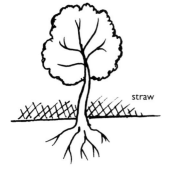

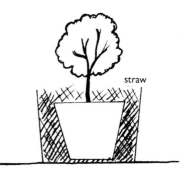

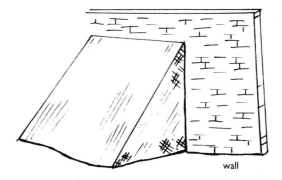

Protecting plants from frost. (i) A straw mulch over the roots. (ii) Straw insulation around the roots, tightly held in by a simple container. (iii) Netting cage constructed to protect wall plants.

Wet

Persistent winter rain, without warm drying sun, will leave containers waterlogged unless some form of overhead canopy is provided.

If there is a roof overhang, it will intercept some of the rain, so move containers closer in to a warm house wall. However, you must ensure they are not going to be splashed with rain water from gutters and downspouts. With immovable containers, you can make individual plastic collars to keep the rain off each plant, but you must remember if you do this to be extra-vigilant as the compost could dry out. Remember, too, that all outdoor containers must overwinter on a free-draining base. Where containerised trees make up an important feature, as with Bonsai and miniature sculptures, it is worth providing a permanent canopy of some sort.

Wind

Wind is a particular danger for young tree and shrub sculptures from late autumn through to late spring, when cold, drying, easterly winds can cause damaging leaf scorch. Continue to protect recently-planted trees and shrubs (especially conifers) by putting up fine mesh netting or lath screens (see below).

Work out some form of shelter for tender-leaved varieties of containerised trees such as Japanese maple, which are extremely vulnerable to wind damage. Similarly, you should do this with any sculpture positioned in the wake of draughty gaps between buildings. In these funnel situations, aim to erect a permeable netting or trellis screen at both ends.

The best long-term answer in windswept gardens is to grow a permanent hedge, or erect a permanent permeable screen or fence. However, you should never attempt to train elaborate topiary feature hedges as the first line of defence.

Sun and Shade

Continue to give evergreens shade from fierce overhead sun (see opposite). Any recently-

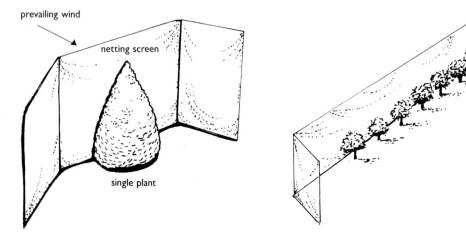

Protecting the plants from wind, with a fine-mesh netting screen supported on a light frame around a newly set-out plant.

prevailing wind

netting screen

single plant

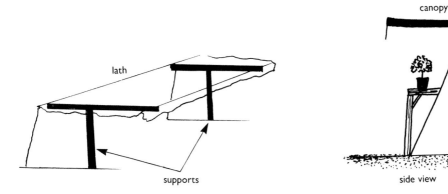

lath

supports

canopy

side view

Protecting plants from snow, sun and rain. This is a shelter for Bonsai and miniature specimens that is very easily built.

planted or potted deciduous sculpture will also benefit from being shaded from the midday sun. Overhead lath or fine mesh netting screens are ideal for summer shading of Bonsai and miniature sculptures.

In over-shaded gardens you can paint dark backgrounds white to reflect the light, if it is practical to do so. Try to thin out branches selectively on large trees where they tend to overshadow smaller specimens.

LIFTING AND OVERWINTERING

Before the onset of autumn frosts (September in cold areas and October in mild), lift and pot up half-hardy herbaceous perennials from their summer beds. Pick over and clean up the plants, removing dead leaves and flowers, and then prune, stake and tie as necessary (see Chapters 5 and 6). The subsequent treatment is largely involved with maintaining suitable overwintering temperatures, and keeping plants out of draughts and the wet.

Plants of 'borderline hardiness', such as antennaria, glechoma, hernieria, sagina and carex, will overwinter successfully under drip- and draught-proof unheated frames. Keep them barely moist, ventilate on fine days, protect from draughts and give extra protection in hard weather.

The rest of the plants under discussion are frost-sensitive and require varying degrees of warmth in a greenhouse or plant room. The hardiest group will survive with a minimum 41°F (5°C) winter temperature. The next group of intermediate plants require 50°F (10°C) minimum, and the most tender plants need temperatures of 60°F (16°C) minimum. See the plant reference section for details on individual plants.

45

4 Pruning

Topiaries and other plant sculptures are totally dependent on pruning for their existence, well-being and success.

REASONS FOR PRUNING

Training, Shaping and Looks

Growers prune and clip plant sculptures in order to train and shape them, and keep their growth within bounds. When the activity is regularly and carefully carried out, plants automatically take on a tidy, well-groomed appearance.

Regulating Growth and Development

By varying the severity, frequency and timing of pruning it is possible to increase or decrease growth rate and vigour at will. Provided it is coupled with correct timing, hard cutting of branches and shoots will normally result in increased vigour, independently of fertiliser applications, but it delays and often diminishes flowering and fruiting. However, although flowers and fruits may be fewer, their size and quality are usually improved. Conversely, light pruning reduces vigour and growth but encourages flowering and fruiting.

In practice, these observations apply mainly to deciduous trees and shrubs, and to a lesser extent to broad-leaved evergreens. Most conifers resent hard cutting and almost always show their disapproval of the practice by dying back.

Keeping Plants Healthy

Correct pruning helps significantly in the battle to keep plants healthy. The prompt cutting out and disposing of diseased shoots and branches removes possible sources of infection, and, by pruning to prevent plant sculptures from growing wider at the top than lower down, air circulation and light will be increased. Consequently, there is less likelihood of any loss of foliage and subsequent bare stems at the base.

Rejuvenation

In the case of old, neglected or damaged sculptures, pruning can sometimes provide the key to rejuvenation and to an extended lease of life. (See the section on renovation work in Chapter 5.)

PRUNING CUTS AND PLANT RESPONSE

When you are caring for plant sculptures, an understanding of how pruning and clipping influence plant growth is bound to be helpful to you.

Apical Dominance

A typical shoot of a new season consists of a terminal or leader bud with a succession of secondary or lateral buds behind. With most trees and shrubs, each terminal bud produces a growth-retarding substance which delays growth in the secondary buds immediately behind it. This regulatory effect of the terminal bud on the lower secondaries is referred to as 'apical dominance'. If you cut off the tip, therefore, the secondary buds will be stimulated into action. The greater the frequency of terminal bud removal, the more bushy the plant will become, and this is nowhere illustrated better than in a clipped hedge.

Basic Pruning Cuts

When you are pruning, it is important to use the cut which is best suited to the situation. The range is wide, from the removal of a single bud to the cutting out of whole branches in extreme cases.

Stopping

This involves the removal of a terminal bud, with the object of promoting bushiness and branching in both woody and soft herbaceous perennials. Pinch out soft tips with the thumbnail, or use a knife or pair of scissors. Either way the bud should be taken out immediately above a leaf joint.

Side-Shooting

Side-shooting is a feature of training single-stem standards, which diverts plant energies up the main stem to the crown. Rub out, with finger and thumb, all secondary buds which are produced in the axils – the space between a leaf stalk and the main stem. Subsequently, you can remove any small side growths which develop from buds which might have been missed.

De-Blossoming and Dead-Heading

De-blossoming is normal on young plants, in certain situations, to prevent exhaustion. Using a knife or scissors you should remove

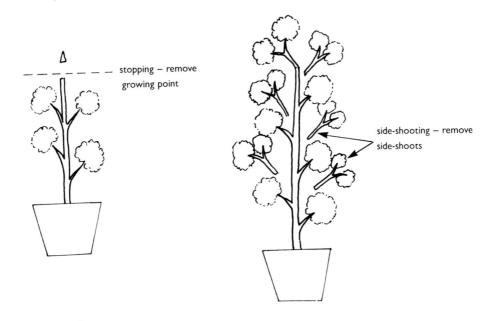

stopping – remove growing point

side-shooting – remove side-shoots

Stopping and side-shooting.

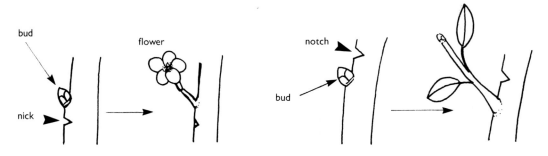

Nicking and notching. Nicking below a bud (in May) lowers vigour and promotes flower bud formation. Notching above a bud stimulates the bud's growth.

flower buds or clusters of flower buds. Dead-heading prevents young or sick plants in particular from overstretching themselves by seed production. It also helps to prolong the flowering period of many half-hardy herbaceous standards. Simply pick off dead and fading flowers.

Nicking and Notching

This technique deserves to be more widely used, especially when pinch and prune sculptures are being trained. Nicking reduces the flow of sap and encourages the formation of flower buds. To do it, you remove a small nick of wood about ½in (1cm) below a growth bud. Notching aims to encourage a dormant growth bud to develop into a shoot, and it should be exploited where bare lengths of stem spoil the sculpture. Cut out a small nick of wood about a third of the way round the stem, just above the dormant growth bud in question.

Clipping, Shearing or Trimming

This is the basic technique used in the formation and maintenance of topiaries. It is normally best carried out regularly, and at short intervals. It is by clipping back the soft tips of new growths that the sought-after, much-branched and dense texture is created. On small features it is normal to use hand shears, but powered clippers will do a good job where you feel the size and scale of the job warrant their use. Have a pair of scissors handy for shaping up miniatures.

Routine Light Pruning

When this is carried out, stems are shortened back to just above a healthy bud. Aim to make a slanting cut starting about ⅛in (3mm) above the bud, sloping slightly downwards and away from it. Use hand pruners for wood up to ½in (1cm) thickness, and to cut thicker wood (up to ¾in (2cm) diameter), use loppers or heavy pruners, otherwise you risk chewing and tearing. Cut back to a good bud or healthy side-shoot. Light pruning is the norm when you are in the process of shaping young sculptures, and is also used to keep mature plants in good condition.

Saw Cuts

These are normally reserved for removing stems and branches of ¾in (2cm) and over.

The Pillar Garden at Hidcote Manor, Gloucestershire, with its enormous clipped yew topiaries.

A peacock and cakestands in yew and box in a small cottage garden at East Lambrook, Somerset.

Container-grown specimens brightening a small front yard at Henley Street, Oxford.

Snow-covered birds on top of a hedge in Kidlington, Oxfordshire.

Amusing clipped subjects near the front porch of a town house in Newcastle.

The tail of this yew peacock forms an effective and attractive archway over the entrance to a well-maintained garden in Kemerton, Gloucestershire.

The knot garden at Barnsley House, Gloucestershire. The tiny hedges of box, *Teucrium chamaedrys* and cotton lavender are clipped in such a way as to appear woven.

These two mature spiral topiaries are an eyecatching feature of the gardens at Westwell Manor, Oxfordshire.

One of six topiary cakestands which sit in the 'Troughery', part of the gardens at Rodmarton Manor in Gloucestershire.

The widespread use of topiary in the Cotswolds was influenced by Gimson and Barnsley and the Arts and Crafts movement, born in Sapperton, Gloucestershire, where these two mature specimens now tower over their small cottage garden.

A flock of plump topiary birds, including a yellow canary, surrounds the pathway in front of this house in Kidlington, Oxfordshire.

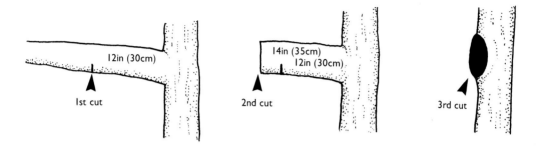

The three-cut method of lopping – the first cut is made on the underside, about one-third of the way through; the second is made downwards and about 2in (5cm) further out from the trunk, while the third cuts the branch off flush with the stem. The wound is then painted with sealant.

However, in topiary and plant sculpture work the saw should only be used as a last resort, to deal with the consequences of old age, neglect, poor management, rot, pests, disease or some other disaster. If the use of a saw is deemed necessary, remove the branch cleanly, back to a main stem, using the 'three cut method' to minimise splitting. Saw about a third of the way through on the underside, about 12in (30cm) out from the main stem. Make a second cut about 2in (5cm) further away from the main stem and cut downwards. Finally, saw off the remaining stump flush with the main stem – don't leave a snag. Smooth off any roughness with a sharp knife. Don't make bigger or more cuts than necessary.

BASIC PRUNING PRACTICE

Always use clean, sharp tools, with moving parts that are well oiled and suitably protected. When you are using powered clippers, wear gloves and goggles in the interests of safety.

Generally speaking, you should prune at the time of year and in the weather conditions best suited to the variety of plant in question

(see individual plant entries in the plant reference section). As a guide, prune or clip evergreens during the warmer months of the year to avoid unsightly wind and frost scorch and die-back. Ideally, you should not prune deciduous trees and shrubs in late winter – this is to minimise the risk of bleeding. Don't attempt to prune while the wood is frosted, as splitting is difficult to avoid under these conditions.

With large-leaved plants, prune out each leaf or stem individually. Never attempt to clip and leave behind segmented leaves – they will only brown at the edges.

All pruning cuts should be clean. Avoid tearing the bark or leaving a 'jagged' finish, and avoid leaving 'snags' – short, blind stubs of stem without a good healthy bud or shoot. They not only look untidy but, most important, they provide entry points for disease as they inevitably die back. You should cut back flush to avoid problems.

Protect all pruning cuts of ¾in (2cm) and over by painting right away with a proprietary pruning sealant.

Never leave prunings lying around. Gather them up and burn them or cart them to the nearest tip. Don't light a fire close to plant

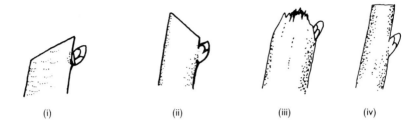

(i)   (ii)   (iii)   (iv)

When making a pruning cut, cut cleanly above a plump bed, slanting the incision away from the bud, as in (i). In (ii), the cut is slanting the wrong way, towards the bud. In (iii), the cut is jagged – this will provide a way in for disease – while in (iv), the cut has been made too high above the bud.

sculptures – if you do this, you will risk severe scorch and lasting damage.

Note Store pruning tools out of harm's way and hold back pruning until young children are safely indoors.

BASIC TRAINING TECHNIQUES

If plant sculptures are to be a success it is vital to maintain their steady growth. When training any plant, no matter how unusual or artificial the ultimate shape, you must never be tempted to deviate from good cultivations (see Chapter 3). To do so is to invite trouble and weak, sickly, unsound plants. The old maxim 'look after the leaves' still holds good. Avoid overcrowding, or robbing the leaves of light in other ways – setting out plant sculptures in dense shade, for instance, is a waste of time. Remember, too, that the overall outline of any sculpture should be wide based, and light and air must get into the lower stems if bareness is to be avoided.

It is also folly to try to train a plant into a shape which is not in character with its natural habit. For example, you should never attempt to train an upright standard into a weeping one – it just won't work.

Training Methods

Traditional Methods

These are inextricably linked with pruning, and in the main complete the job started during the initial pruning process. Pruning is used to form the basic framework which is then moulded into shape by bending, tying in and supporting into position. However, it isn't as straightforward as this, and the skilled plantsman makes good use of the various effects on growth and bud development as branch or shoot positions are altered.

It is well known that in the case of upright trees and shrubs, shoots and branches trained vertically upwards put most of their energy into excessive growth at the tip. Horizontally-trained branches encourage more even growth along the full length, and, where appropriate, promote flowering and fruiting. Finally, if branches are trained downwards they produce weak growth at the tips.

Budding and Grafting

It is not suggested that intending topiarists or plant sculpturists need to start budding or grafting, but they should be aware that plants such as weeping cotoneaster and weeping willows cannot be grown as standards without budding or grafting on to rootstocks of closely related standard varieties. Unless you are an experienced grower, it is best to buy in ready-budded or ready-grafted stock.

One point to watch when buying crab apple, flowering cherry or flowering plum is that, within broad limits, the ultimate size of tree can be determined. Select trees on dwarf, medium or vigorous rootstocks, as appropriate.

In extreme cases, given experienced hands, it is possible to bud or graft new shoots successfully on to otherwise bare stems.

Chemicals

These serve a role as an aid to training, and growth regulators are the main group of chemicals currently on sale, which are likely to influence gardening in the near future. The use of these chemicals is as yet in its infancy amongst amateurs, but it does seem set to take off, and every gardener should watch developments in this area.

Growth regulators operate in various ways, and they range from growth accelerators, as with gibberellins, to retardants such as cycocel and maleic hydrazide. It is the retardants which have so far shown greatest promise. They hold back shoot extension and at the same time encourage side-shoot growth and branching. They are being increasingly used by commercial growers to dwarf pot plants, and they could have a part to play with miniature sculptures. Early indications are that growth retardants also show promising possibilities when it comes to maintaining mature topiary hedges with the minimum of cutting.

At the present time growth regulators are mostly applied as foliar sprays to mature plants. Some retardants are suitable for incorporating into the potting compost when potting up young plants, and this is the common practice with the majority of commercial growers.

5   Topiary Techniques

The pruning and training of topiaries must be geared to suit the age and the condition of the plant. For example, formation training must be undertaken on young plants, mature topiary features have to be given routine treatment, while remedial or rejuvenation measures need to be taken to revive old, neglected or damaged topiaries.

FORMATION TRAINING

The secret of success with any form of topiary is to start with suitable, sturdy, well-furnished plants, with all-round branching and foliage down to soil level. The importance of good all-round cladding from the ground upwards cannot be stressed too strongly if bareness at the base is to be avoided. The plants should also be young. The reason for this is that young wood breaks away more freely and more readily when it is clipped and pruned than older wood which is invariably harder.

The shaping and training of topiary features should start at the earliest practical time – as soon as the plants are big enough to handle – and every effort should be made to encourage steady but strong, vigorous growth during the early formative years. The other ingredient for success is patience. For example, you should allow about five years to create a simple box or evergreen honeysuckle topiary, and about ten for the same thing in yew. More ambitious shapes can easily take twice as long, needing up to fifteen years and more to be completed.

Once plants of suitable varieties are growing freely, no matter whether in well-prepared ground or containers, and routine care is of the highest standard, then training can begin. (*See* plant reference section for lists of suitable varieties.)

Simple Specimen Topiaries

These make an excellent starting point for anyone who may be new to topiary work. Begin with a single plant or a small grouping of three plants (preferred by some topiarists), and allow to grow unchecked until 8–12in (20–30cm) of new growth has been put on. Quick-growing evergreen honeysuckle, privet and hornbeam should have done this by midsummer during the first season after planting, and slower-growing box and yew by the following year. At this stage you should cut the plants back by about half, dealing with broad-leaved evergreens in midsummer but holding back on deciduous kinds until autumn. Do not top conifers – they should be allowed to grow on until the ultimate height of feature is reached. Lightly clip in the sides of all plants (including conifers), taking back the new growth by no more than about a quarter, and thereafter, cut back vertical shoots, by about a third to a half, each time 6–8in (15–20cm) of new growth is made. Lightly clip in the sides as before at the same time. Where the aim is to create tall, narrow, pyramidal or columnar sculptures, selective thinning out of the top growth will very often be necessary. You will also need to cut in the sides a little more severely near the top to give a tapered effect.

After four or five trimmings, the plants

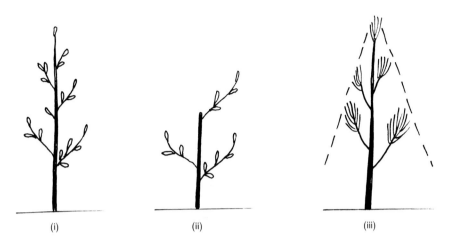

Training a topiary specimen. (i) Allow broad-leaved plants to grow
8–12in (20–30cm) unchecked, and then cut back by half. (ii) Allow
conifers to grow up unchecked to the required height, clipping only the
sides.

should be ready to withstand serious 'cutting
to shape'. If you have a good eye and a steady
hand, simple shapes such as globes, cubes,
pyramids, columns, cones and domed
features should not present any very great
problems.

Miniature Sculptures

Training of miniature sculptures follows
broadly similar lines to simple specimen
topiaries, although on a smaller scale. The
same basic range of shapes can be adapted.
Cut back initially when 4–6in (10–15cm) of top
growth has been made, and subsequently cut
at every 2in (5cm) or so of growth. Clip in the
sides lightly at the same time – very much in
the same way that you would do with their
larger cousins.

Traditional Topiary Standards

With time and patience, the growing and
training of topiary standards is well within the

reach of those who are prepared to make the
effort and to pay attention to the necessary
detail. The training of any standard is a two-
part operation. The first stage is to form a
strong, straight stem capable of supporting
and sustaining the crown, and the second
stage is to develop and shape the crown.

Forming the Stem

The training of woody-stemmed, free-
standing topiary standards is more or less
similar for most plants, and for container-
grown as well as for direct-planted stock.
Relatively minor variations from variety to
variety are referred to as and when it is
necessary.

During the critical stem formation period –
which may be anything from 1 to 3 years – you
should give standards the best possible care.
This is to encourage the sort of strong growth
that is vital for a good stem (also known as the
'leg' or 'shank'). Stake and then tie at 4–6in
(10–15cm) intervals. Use one cane per plant

53

and tie with soft twine, taking care not to chafe or damage the bark, and don't tie too tight or sap flow will be interrupted – allow for stem expansion. Take the twine twice round the cane and once round the stem to avoid slippage. The alternative is to use proprietary plastic ties – in fact, they are probably more reliable.

Those who have trained standard geraniums and fuchsias will be used to taking out the buds or side-shoots as soon as they are big enough to handle. *Don't* do this with woody-stemmed standards. Instead, you should allow each side-shoot to form 4–6 leaves before pinching out its growing point. However, do remove any suckers which arise from below the ground as soon as they

become evident, and do this right back to their point of origin. When the desired height of clear stem is reached, allow the main leader to continue for a further 8–12in (20–30cm) before stopping. The usual length of clear stem to allow for topiary standards varies from about 3½–5ft (1–1.5m), the measurement being taken from soil level to the lowest branch at the base of the crown. The four-leaved side-shoots are left on the lower part of the stem for one or two years, with the object of thickening and strengthening the stem, which they do very effectively. Shorten any secondary side-shoots back to a pair of leaves as they arise.

After one or two years have elapsed, clean up the stem, from ground to crown base,

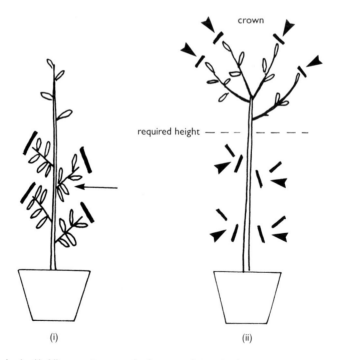

Training topiary standards. (i) Allow topiary standards to reach required height before stopping, pinching each side-shoot at 4–6 leaves. (ii) When stem is thick enough and tall enough, cut off side-shoots below required clear stem height. Clip crown shoots to give bushiness.

using a very sharp pruning knife or a good pair of pruners. The actual timing of this operation will depend on the appearance and thickness of the stem, and whether it looks strong enough for the crown and is in proportion with it. One useful consequence of cutting off the lower side-shoots is an upsurge of energy and growth in the crown.

Shaping the Crown

The central main stem is allowed to grow to another 8–12in (20–30cm) beyond the required length of clear stem, therefore, before it is stopped. Side-shoots arising in the topmost 8–12in (20–30cm) are not pinched at the four-leaf stage, but are left to grow on for a time.

With some trees (for example, holly and bay), side-shoots are produced with a wide crotch – that is to say, they are set at a wide angle to their main stem. With these trees and shrubs routine clipping can begin without any further preliminary training. Make a start as soon as it is practical – in other words, once shoots have put on 6–8in (15–20cm) of growth.

The side-shoots of topiary plants such as box and cotoneaster often form a narrow crotch (a narrow angle with the main stem). These are more likely to snap off later in life, during high winds or after heavy falls of snow, and their upswept branches are also more likely to become prematurely bare at the base than those of, for example, holly and bay, with their more naturally horizontal habit. The ideal remedy is to train the lower branches at the base of the crown while they are still young and pliant. If you delay, they are likely to become brittle and stiff. Attach a circular wire frame of about 8in (20cm) in diameter, to the supporting cane. Lay it horizontally around the base of the intended crown, and adjust the wire height carefully so that it is within reach of the lower shoots without the need to bend them downwards. As soon as the lowest shoots are long enough – they need to be at least 6in (15cm) – gently bend six or eight of them as near to the vertical as possible, without breaking them or kinking them. Then tie each shoot in turn to the circle of wire, spacing them evenly around it, so that they look like the spokes of a wheel. Remove the growing points from these shoots when they have made another 6–8in (15–20cm) of growth, and shorten back the remainder of untied shoots by about a third at the same time. Subsequently, clip after each 6–8in (15–20cm) of growth is made.

About a year after training and tying in the lower shoots, you can remove the ties and wires. By this time the wood should have ripened and the shoots are unlikely to spring back into the narrow crotch position.

Fashion the standards as they grow by clipping. With imagination, crowns can take on a variety of shapes, but, to begin with, balls, ovals or lollipops, cones and pyramids are amongst the easiest to effect.

Once the shape and outline have been established, routine maintenance can begin.

Miniature Standards

The procedure for training miniature standards is very similar to that outlined for traditional standards, with the difference that it is usual for all miniatures to be grown and trained in containers. Since they are smaller than traditional standards, the time it takes to establish a trained miniature from start is appreciably shorter. Results can, in many cases, be achieved in 5–7 years, as opposed to the 10–15 years needed for traditional topiary standards.

Forming the Stem

The main stem is allowed to grow unstopped until the required length of clear stem – plus a bit extra – is attained. (In the case of miniatures this usually varies from about 6–16in (15–40cm). Unlike traditional topiary standards the buds or emerging side-shoots are removed as soon as they are large enough to deal with. Thick stems are neither necessary nor desirable, and would be out of proportion to the overall topiary. A small pair of pointed scissors will ease the task of cutting out side-shoots.

Shaping the Crown

The main central stem is allowed to grow a further 2–4in (5–10cm) beyond the required length of clear stem, and is then stopped. It is usual to cut 1–2in (3–5cm) off the top, with the object of making the crown bush out. Allow the resulting new shoots to grow 2–4in (5–10cm), then clip to shorten them by half, removing 1–2in (3–5cm) off each tip. Gradually the crown is shaped with each successive clipping.

Advanced Topiary Specimens

To the untutored eye, there may not appear to be much to distinguish simple topiary specimens from the more intricate forms of spirals, birds and animals, especially when they are seen from a distance. However, when it comes to training there is a great deal of difference. Simple specimen topiaries are easy enough for most beginners to tackle (see page 52), but a certain amount of know-how is needed for the more elaborate shapes. Remember that much of the graft and many hours can be saved – and mistakes and disappointments avoided – if a durable wire or metal frame is used. In fact, only the most experienced of topiarists can manage without one.

Making the Foundation

As a general rule, it is easier, and there is less risk of damage, to put the framework in place *before* planting. Unfortunately, this is not always practical. The plants may already be set out, or perhaps the topiary feature is to be superimposed on an existing hedge.

The **corkscrew** or **spiral** is one of the easiest of the intricate forms, and therefore one of the best to start off with. It is well suited to both container growing and direct planting.

One highly successful spiral foundation frame can be created by pushing a thin solid or tubular metal stake vertically into the ground, positioning it centrally beside the plant (see diagram). Make sure that it is firm enough as well as tall enough to accommodate the mature spiral. Don't attempt to grow a spiral any higher than 3½–4ft (1–1.2m), as it would be likely to take too long to grow over and cover successfully. In practice this means starting off with a metal stake about 5–6ft (1.2–1.8m) long, allowing 18in (45cm) below ground for stability. The stake must not be too thick – anything over ½in (1cm) in diameter could look ugly. Once the stake is hammered home, fix three galvanised wire rings to it. They should be of about 12 gauge and, say, 12in, 9in and 6in (30, 23 and 15cm) in diameter respectively, assuming a 3½ft (1m) high spiral. Set the largest circle horizontally about 10in (25cm) above soil level, with the other two spaced a similar distance apart, one above the other, and securing the smallest circle on top. Then using more 12-gauge wire, fashion a tapering spiral coil, tying it to each wire circle as it coils its way up to the top of the stake.

In the case of **animal shapes** the procedure is slightly different. Using similar wire, fashion the outline of the animal – a fox, a peacock or

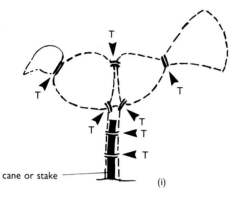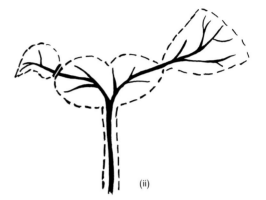

Training a topiary shape on a foundation frame. (i) Make a wire frame (for example, a bird, as shown here), tying at points shown 'T'. Use tie wire and support on a cane or stake. (ii) Train out, tying in if necessary the branch framework to fill the frame. Clip to shape, filling out the sides.

maybe a fish are some ideas – but don't make it any longer than 3ft (90cm) and of a height in proportion. Hold the outline foundation in position by wiring to two suitably placed vertical metal stakes (use thinner wire of 14- to 16-gauge). This should make the job easier. Where topiaries are to be grown on top of a hedge, use heavier stakes (say ¾in (2cm)) as stilts. These will be concealed within the hedge (see diagram). The thinner stakes supporting the foundation framework are then attached to the stilts. Finally, neaten off by cutting back any protruding stakes.

Scaled-down frames can easily be made, using a little ingenuity and imagination, if you are interested in growing miniatures.

Shaping the Plants

Having fashioned a foundation to suit both the site and personal inclination, the next stage is training the plants.

Calculate on a minimum of one plant per spiral and two per animal, and never be tempted to train conifers into intricate forms – yew is the only notable exception to this rule. (See plant reference section for suitable plants.)

Encourage strong growth by giving your plants every assistance with watering, feeding and shelter. Allow them to make about 12in (30cm) of new vertical growth, and then cut each of them back by half – this will encourage strong shoots to break away from the base. Don't be tempted to delay cutting back, allowing plants to grow taller in an effort to save time. It is a false economy and involves the subsequent risk of bare stems at the base of the sculpture.

Concentrate on the new shoots which arise. Select four of the strongest on each plant and allow them to grow about 10–12in (25–30cm) vertically, before tying them down. Bend three down almost horizontally and tie them in to the foundation, after shortening them back by approximately one-third. The fourth, or 'frame', stem is similarly shortened, but allowed to grow vertically upwards. All the other new shoots — in other words, those remaining after the four strongest were selected — are cut back by half as soon as 4–6in (10–15cm) of growth has been made.

Treatment of subsequent 'frame' stems is a repeat of the above procedure, and this continues until the framework of main branches covers the wire frame. All other shoots are cut back by half each time 4–6in (10–15cm) of growth has been made. This allows the topiary to extend outwards by about 4in (10cm) at each pruning, so encouraging it to cover the wire eventually.

Once the main foundation frame is covered and suitably shaped, routine clipping can begin.

With **tall topiaries** such as **the hedge and the arch** where the aim is to achieve a typical clipped green wall effect, the training process is fairly straightforward, and follows similar lines to that required for simple specimen topiaries (see page 52). Set out a double row of hedging plants at the recommended planting distances for the specific variety. Where buttresses are to be used as a feature, make provision for training by setting out a couple of extra plants for each buttress. Subsequent training would then be in proportion to the scale of the hedge.

Much of the beauty of a clipped green wall lies in the effect of an even, balanced growth from one end to the other. It is therefore imperative that, by good care and attention to detail, strong healthy growth is promoted during the early formative years. It is equally important that the edge should be protected from passers-by, and from animals and pests for that matter, and you should note that those running alongside paths and other hard-surfaced areas are most at risk. Accidents to young hedges can, and do, result in unsightly gaps — especially where bicycles are involved,

for example. Very often you will need some form of physical barrier. A wire netting or chain-link fence erected on the vulnerable side should suffice, but remember that it must be spaced sufficiently far out to allow for pruning — about 2ft (60cm) would be the minimum. If you find it visually unacceptable, chestnut paling fencing is a little better, and can be erected on a temporary basis for a few years. Take care not to use anything which might obstruct light, and be sure to use strong enough stakes, at intervals no more than 7ft (2m) apart.

When it comes to training **topiary archways** there are several ways of tackling the job. The approach depends, in part at least, on the siting of the arch, and whether it is part of a continuous hedge or free-standing. Wherever an arch is planned, a metal foundation is strongly recommended. The easiest way is to purchase one ready-made, but quite honestly the handyman won't be too troubled making one up himself. It is essential that the foundation frame should be well anchored, as any movement in a high wind could be disastrous.

Where the arch is set in hedging, it is normally best to let the plants reach their final hedge height before starting on the overhead arch itself. (Treatment up to this point should follow that outlined in the section on hedging.) The up-and-over part of the arch above hedge height is then trained as follows. Allow the plants at either side of the archway to grow up vertically 12in (30cm), before shortening back by about a third. Tie in. Encourage the plants to make another 12in (30cm) of growth, and then shorten them back and tie in as before. Repeat the process, arching over and tying in over the top, until the two sides meet and intermesh.

In the case of a free-standing arch the training outlined above starts almost from ground level — with one exception. The first cut of the young hedge plants, when they are

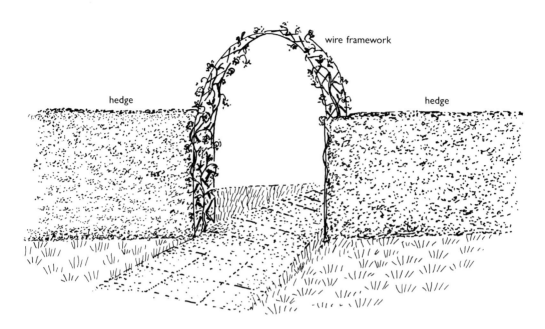

To create a topiary arch, train and clip plants over a sturdy frame.

12in (30cm) high, is to reduce their height by half. Thereafter, new growths are cut back by one-third as above.

When both sides of the arch have been intermeshed, you can move on to routine clipping.

Pleached trees are trained and kept in shape in one of two ways – either by clipping alone, or by a combination of clipping and pruning. Provided easy subjects such as beech and hornbeam are selected, clipping on its own is adequate, but when more demanding trees such as lime are used, then the clip and prune technique is called for.

The *clipped method* is fairly common. Start by planting two parallel rows of trees, 'avenue fashion', with a pathway in between. The trees are normally allowed to grow vertically, unchecked, until 6–12in (15–30cm) above the required height of clear stem, which is somewhere between 3½ and 7ft (1–2.5m). Then training begins. (However, if growth is

sluggish after planting, you should cut the young trees back almost to ground level in the autumn, 6 to 12 months after setting them out. This has the long-term effect of speeding up growth.)

Start training by clipping about 4in (10cm) off the tops. Allow fresh shoots to make about 12in (30cm) of vertical growth, then clip them back by about one-third. Continue the process until the ultimate height is reached – this is normally 7–10ft (2–3m) from the ground. The side growths are treated in much the same way as a hedge. After the 'head' has been clipped two or three times, clean up the trunks in the same sort of way as you would with the standards.

Clip and prune pleaching is a method of training normally reserved for widely-spaced lime trees, planted about 7–10ft (2–3m) apart. When the trees are tall enough, you should cut the main stems back to about 4in (10cm) above the level of the bottom branches

– again, this is from 3½–7ft (1–2m). Do this in the autumn. Allow three strong shoots to grow out from the top, and then summer prune all the others back to three leaves. These three shoots are subsequently trained to produce an espalier type of framework, with pairs of horizontal main branches 12–16in (30–40cm) apart, supported on wires (see page 80). Don't allow the new shoots which arise from the espalier arms to make more than about 10in (25cm) of growth before tipping them back during the summer. This creates the traditional 'hedge-on-stilts' effect. Once the bottom espalier tier is formed, start cleaning up the trunk. Cut out all side growths cleanly and flush with the main trunk, right up to the bottom branch level. This is a job which should be done in the autumn each year.

Limit the tree's growth to a convenient height of, say, 10ft (3m) maximum, then begin routine pruning.

Low topiary edgings, divisions and **ground cover** have long been in vogue (see page 11 on knot gardens and parterres), and are not too difficult to create effectively.

The very essence of a good edging or divider is a dense, tight texture, and the key to success is frequent and regular close clipping. Broad-leaved evergreen shrubs are usually the most successful plants to try. Allow foliage shrubs such as dwarf box to grow about 4–6in (10–15cm) after planting, and then cut them back by about half. Subsequently, cut each time 1in (3cm) of growth is made, shortening back by ½in (1cm). It is very important to follow the 'wide-based, narrow top' principle to prevent snow damage and spreading, as well as to ensure good leafage down to soil level. With flowering shrubs such as heathers, lavender and rosemary, clip frequently for a tight texture. Otherwise, if flowers are a priority, clip annually for a looser effect, and use these plants for edgings rather than for divisions.

With **wall topiary,** regardless of whether climbers or wall shrubs are used, formation training is a two-stage operation. Stage one is the provision and erection of supports on to which plants are trained, while stage two is all about forming and shaping the main framework of stems and branches.

Supporting wall topiary is a priority (see pages 26–27). When you are dealing with climbers, especially those with a self-clinging habit, such as ivy, always aim to use trellis. This should be fixed to a light framework of treated timber or rust-proof metal, and set a minimum 1in (3cm) out from the wall. This is to prevent any rooting into the wall with consequential damage. The increased air flow also has the beneficial effect of drying off surplus moisture, which can otherwise become a hazard, particularly where old walls are concerned. An arrangement of straining wires supported on vine eyes is a convenient way to support wall shrubs such as pyracantha.

Forming the framework of plants which are maintained strictly by clipping (for example, climbers such as ivy) is usually a question of pushing in two or three short canes, splayed out. This provides the stems with a bridge to lead them on to the bottom of the trellis. Thereafter, it is largely a matter of training out the main stems, fan-wise, and tying them in as necessary. Clip back any shoots which grow out away from the wall at right angles, and don't allow the plants to make more than 6–8in (15–20cm) of growth before shortening them back by half to two-thirds. If any of the main stem looks like growing away at the expense of the others, clip back their tips. Otherwise, allow the climbers to cover their allotted wall space, and then start routine maintenance clipping.

Wall plants such as pyracantha and cotoneaster (suitable varieties only) should be trained fan-wise as cordons or espaliers to provide the main framework. (See pages 78–80 for details.) During training, clip to shape the secondary growths, shortening them back by half, or more, whenever 2–4in (5–10cm) of growth is made. As with climbers, routine clipping takes over when the plant has filled its allotted space.

ROUTINE MAINTENANCE

Once the framework of main branches and secondary shoots is established, your aim should be to restrain growth and so maintain the topiary in good shape.

Clipping

The guiding principle with good routine care is to cut little and often during the growing season. Both evergreen and deciduous plants are clipped as necessary between April and September – topiaries in exposed gardens in cold districts are the exception. In these cases, you should delay clipping until May, otherwise you risk scorch from freezing winds in a late spring. Stop in early September, so that the cuts have a chance to heal and seal before the onset of winter.

When you are dealing with traditional, free-standing specimens, or with topiary hedges and arches, the guideline is to clip whenever 2–4in (5–10cm) of growth is made, shortening the new shoots back to within about ½in (1cm) of the old growth. It is this hard cutting which ensures that you will achieve the sought-after, dense, close texture. The growth rate of the plant in question will determine how often the topiary needs clipping (see details on individual plants), but, as a rough guide, quick growers such as evergreen honeysuckle will require clipping every 3 weeks or so; slow-growers such as box, and yew once it is established, will only need clipping two or three times during the growing season. When

you are clipping, you should always aim to keep the tops of the topiaries narrower than the base – this is vital with free-standing features. When you are clipping long horizontal or vertical stretches of topiary, such as hedges, a wavy or ragged effect can be largely avoided by using a guide of some sort. A straight edge is ideal, but a piece of light-coloured string held taut between two points will suffice.

The guidelines for routine care of pleaching are broadly similar, except that you can allow the shoots to make up to 6in (15cm) of growth before clipping them.

Suckers and Side-Growths

With standard and specimen topiary features, and pleaching, you must keep the base and stem clear of suckers and side-growths. If they are cut out cleanly with a sharp knife flush with the stem, or back to the point of origin at the base, regrowth is less likely than if a short stump is left.

Miniature Topiary

The general guidelines are much the same – cut little and often. In the case of miniatures, this means whenever ½–¾in (1–2cm) of growth is made. The shoots should be shortened back to within about ¼in (6mm) of the old growth. You will find that scissors are much more handy than shears for this small-scale work.

Edgings and Ground Cover

Routine care should be varied according to the main attraction of the plants involved – in other words, whether they are grown for their flowers or their foliage. Foliage edgings and ground cover are neatened as soon as they begin to get untidy, and this is usually when no more than 2–3in (5–8cm) of growth has been made. Clip new top and side growths back to within ½in (1cm) of the older wood. Flowering plants such as heathers, no matter whether they are used as edgings or ground cover, are normally clipped only once annually, just after flowering. However, with late summer-flowering varieties of heathers and similar plants, you should delay clipping until the spring. To clip more often than once annually would be to forego much of the flower colour and interest.

Wall Tracery

When climbers and wall shrubs are treated as topiary features, they must be clipped round the sides and at the top to restrict height and width, so that they remain in keeping with their surroundings. Do not allow them to put on more than 6in (15cm) of new growth before shortening them back by a half to two-thirds.

With summer-flowering and fruiting wall shrubs such as pyracantha and cotoneaster, three clippings will normally suffice. Give the first cut when flowering is almost over, some time in June. Carry out the second cut when the berries have formed with some starting to colour up – about early to mid-August. Then give the third and final trim some time early in September to tidy up the plants for winter.

RENOVATIONS AND REPAIRS

The hallmark of perfection in topiary is an even, close texture devoid of holes, gaps and bare stems. Unfortunately, it is not uncommon to be faced with these problems, and they are the result very often of pests, diseases or accident. In extreme cases an entire plant may succumb and die out.

Holes

Where holes are due to the death of the specimen, you must dig out the affected plant promptly, lifting it with as much of its old soil as possible. Gently tease out some of the soil from around the roots of adjoining plants making up the topiary feature, but don't be too ruthless. Replace with fresh potting compost, and set out a new container-grown plant at the time of year best suited to the individual variety.

Gaps

These can arise at almost any time, and covering them up need not be too difficult, provided they are caught in time. One of the best ways to deal with this situation is to train another shoot or shoots into the gap. If it is obvious that no existing shoot is long enough to fill the gap, then set about training a replacement shoot or shoots. Allow one or two suitably placed shoots to grow 8–12in (20–30cm) in length. Shorten them back by a third or more, and then tie them into the gap. If the gap is rather large, tie in place some wire mesh netting as a foundation over which to train the new shoots. The resulting new side-shoots are then clipped as described under routine management (see page 61).

It is feasible to apply basic hole and gap filling to most forms of topiary, as long as you give it a little thought.

Bare Stems

It is never easy to cover up bare stems, but it is often possible to adapt the replacement shoot method outlined above. When doing this, try to avoid tying in replacement shoots below the level of the horizontal – this should only be done as a last resort. Plants will need nursing afterwards if weak growths are to be

avoided. A better alternative is often to set out a young, vigorous plant close in, and then to train it up to cover the bare stems.

Renewal

With topiary wall shrubs, disease and old age can take their toll, and a replacement framework of branches may be called for. The procedure is usually fairly straightforward. If an existing branch is rotten, you should cut it out, right back to sound wood. Then you can tie in a new shoot as described under formation training. If a branch is past its prime, but has some useful life remaining, leave it. Continue routine maintenance and, at the same time, train up a new replacement shoot. Once the replacement shoot has made enough growth, cut out the old stem and tie in the new.

Neglected and Overgrown Plants

The main problem for the topiarist here is to decide if the topiary is beyond the point of no return. Where a topiary feature is neglected and out of shape, with bare stems, and has several seasons' worth of uncut growth, you should really grub it out and start again.

If the neglect is not too serious, with perhaps only a year's uncut growth, then fairly hard cutting back, plus replacement shoot growth, can work wonders. When you are cutting back, bear in mind it is important not to cut back into old wood with evergreens.

When topiary is neglected and overgrown, invariably other trees and shrubs will be in a similar state. Where overhead branches form a dense canopy, thin them out to allow more light and air to reach the topiary.

6 Pinch and Prune Sculptures

Plants which are trained and subsequently maintained by pinching and pruning have, for convenience's sake, and the benefit of the reader, been grouped into two classes – soft-stemmed and woody plants. The first part of the chapter deals with the detailed training and care of soft-stemmed or semi soft-stemmed plants, such as geraniums and fuchsias, while in the second part woody plants are discussed. (*See* plant guide for lists of plants for specific purposes.)

TRAINING SOFT-STEMMED SCULPTURES

Standards

The traditional idea of a standard is a head or crown of branching stems on top of a single main stem. In this *specialist* field of training, however, standards are described variously as 'short', 'half-standard' and 'full standard', depending on the length of clean stem between soil level and the lowest branches. For average garden purposes, there is no need to be too precise, but the potential exhibitor should check any show schedule thoroughly to avoid disqualification on points of technicality.

Success with standards, and other pinch and prune sculptures, depends in good measure on healthly, vigorous growth. This is particularly important during the formative training period, when any set-back to growth or plant health can ruin your chances of producing a top-quality standard. Because of the soft nature of the stem, the tallest full and half standards are best grown and trained indoors. This is essential in cold areas where undue hardening of the stems is almost inevitable, resulting in stunting which, in turn, prevents the rapid growth necessary to produce bushy, well-branched crowns.

The training of any standard is a two-part operation, involving firstly stem building, and secondly crown formation.

Stem Building

Your aim should be to produce a strong, straight stem of even thickness from soil level up to the crown in a *single* growing season – this is the crunch! The objective is not difficult to achieve in the case of a short standard with a clear 12in (30cm) stem, but more care and know-how will be needed to produce half standards with stems of 18–24in (45–60cm), and full standards, with stems of 30in (75cm) plus, will be the most demanding of all. Don't fall into the trap of growing the stem over two years, as the result is likely to be a crooked stem of uneven thickness.

Start with a strong, upright-growing, suitable variety. (Pendulous and weeping kinds are unsuitable for stem building purposes.) Be sure to use healthy plants which are free of any sign of deformity, unusual leaf mottling or stunting – these are all symptoms of virus diseases.

Timing is important, especially with regards

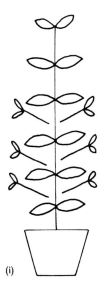

(i)

to propagation and its subsequent effect on training. For instance the traditional practice of rooting geraniums in June or early July for training as full standards still holds good, and with fuchsias, cuttings struck in August or early September usually do well. (*See* details on individual plants for guidance on other standards.) Pot up rooted cuttings singly into 5in (13cm) pots before they become pot-bound. The secret of stem elongation (without using chemicals) is to keep the rooted cuttings growing steadily in warmth, through the winter. Aim to maintain a minimum 50°F (10°C) for geraniums, or 58°F (14°C) minimum for fuchsias, and give maximum winter light. (It *is* possible to hasten stem elongation by using growth-promoting chemicals such as gibberellins, but opinions are very

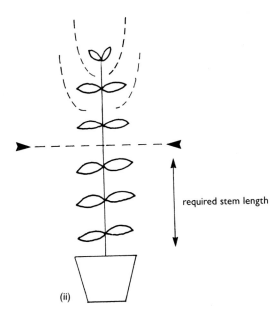

(ii)

required stem length

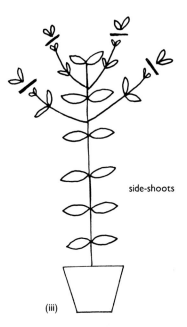

side-shoots

(iii)

Training a soft-stemmed standard. (i) For the stem building, remove the side-shoots as they arise, until the required length of clear stem is achieved. (ii) Remove the growing point high enough above the required stem height to allow 4–6 side-shoots to develop at the top. (iii) Pinch out the side-shoot tips so that a bushy crown is formed.

much divided on their benefits. Thin, weak, spindly stems are not unknown following their application, and, in any event, excellent results are obtainable without their assistance.)

Stake plants individually, from their first potting onwards. Use split canes and tie in each stem every 2in (5cm) or so. In February, as soon as the days lengthen noticeably, pot on into 8in (20cm) containers before the roots become matted in the 5in (13cm) pots. Restake with a longer cane to support the growing stem, and continue to tie in as before. With the onset of longer days, increase watering and create humidity on fine, warm days by damping down generally, and misting over plants such as fuchsias. Increase ventilation during the spring and summer and shade plants from strong overhead sun. Don't neglect liquid feeding either – this should start three weeks after the final potting, and should be continued until September.

Side-Shooting and Stopping

One of the most important jobs when stem building is the prompt and regular removal of side-shoots. This should be done as soon as they are large enough to handle. In this way, nutrients and energy are diverted to the growing point, and ultimately to the crown.

Once the plant has formed the required height of stem, you should not remove any more side-shoots. Allow another six leaves to develop, then pinch out the main growing point.

This guide to side-shooting and stopping applies to most traditional standards.

Crown Formation

A minimum of four good side-shoots are needed to provide the main crown framework. Although six leaves are allowed to develop before stopping, rarely do six good

side-shoots arise. Pinch out the two weakest, and allow the others to grow on until they are 2–3in (5–8cm) long, then pinch out the growing point immediately beyond a leaf. Subsequently, stop the resultant secondary side-shoots when they are 2in (5cm) in length. This is to encourage bushiness.

With half and full standards, the development and training of the crown is carried out mainly in the year following stem building. With short standards, the stem and the crown can often be produced in a single year.

Multi-stemmed Standards

Multi-stemmed standards have proved to be very popular in parts of the USA, but as yet they are not grown to any great extent in Britain. They deserve a wider recognition. Unlike normal standards, the multi-stem variation is made up of several plants, usually of a climbing habit – ivy is very useful for the purpose. The same guidelines apply as with any standard when it comes to growing and shaping indoors to maintain the sort of steady growth which is embodied in good care and cultivation. Thereafter, one very satisfactory way to tackle the job of training is as follows.

Stem Building

During July or early August, root six to eight ivy cuttings, spacing them evenly around the edge of a 3½in (9cm) pot, either indoors or under a frame. To ensure an even batch, and to avoid the situation where one or two over-vigorous plants grow away at the expense of others, grade the cuttings for even size. Also, try to stick to one variety or, alternatively, use varieties of equal vigour.

Move the cuttings *en bloc* into a 5in (13cm) pot when they have rooted, without waiting for them to get matted or pot-bound. Push a single split cane into the centre and train the

stems up the cane, tying in gently but firmly at 2in (5cm) intervals. Keep the plants growing steadily through winter at 45–50°F (7–10°C) minimum for the quickest and best results. Plants overwintered at 40°F (5°C) will be slower to grow and less leafy by spring than those kept at the higher temperatures. However, unlike single stem standards, they will not suffer unduly at lower temperatures.

In the spring, pot on from 5in (13cm) into 7in (18cm) containers with minimum disturbance to roots and plants. Never allow plants to become pot-bound. Replace the split cane with a slightly heavier support, standing at least 2ft (60cm) above soil level. As soon as most of the stems are about 2ft (60cm) high, make a start on training the crown. Taller multi-stem standards are possible, but the main disadvantage is that it takes longer to train them.

Side-Shooting

Apart from limiting each plant to a single main stem by removing the side growths (most of which break away at the base), little side-shooting is needed during stem building in the first year.

Crown Formation

Attach a small 10in (25cm) diameter rose tree trainer to the top of the cane some 2–2½ft (60–75cm) above the rim of the pot. These trainers look rather like an inverted wire-framed hanging basket. Encourage the stems of the ivy – or other climber – to grow up through the centre of the trainer and spill over the frame. Meanwhile the stems below trainer level must be kept tied in to the cane, and, in the second and subsequent years, all

cane

rose-trainer

(i)   (ii)

Training a multi-stemmed standard. (i) Train several stems of a plant such as ivy up a cane. (ii) Train the stems down over a rose trainer when they are tall enough.

additional side-shoots which arise from the main stem between soil level and the crown should be carefully cut out to maintain a clear multi-stem. Spread the stems out evenly over the trainer, and tie each one in separately to keep it in place. The stems will trail and cascade down from the trainer frame. Shorten them back as necessary to prevent them dropping any lower than about 6in (15cm) below the rim of the frame, and thin out overcrowded side-shoots at the same time.

Pyramids

Various plants, especially those like fuchsias, look particularly attractive when they are trained and grown as pyramids. As with standards, the best results are obtained by growing them indoors during the training period. Similar first-rate growing conditions, without set-backs, are necessary if good, well-shaped plants are to be obtained quickly. In the training of pyramids the matter of size is less clear-cut than with standards. For practical purposes, height is determined partly by varietal vigour, and partly by the amount of growth made during the first season – all this is geared to the excellence or otherwise of plant management and care.

Pyramid training is carried out in two stages – firstly, frame building, followed by pinching to thicken up the foliage.

Frame Building

As with standards, dwarf specimens make less exacting demands, and require a less high standard of management than their taller counterparts. If you are aiming to grow the largest specimens (upwards of 4–5ft (1.2–1.5m) in height), your starting point is cuttings struck in July or early August. Root the cuttings indoors in warm, lightly-shaded conditions, and pot up, when they are rooted,

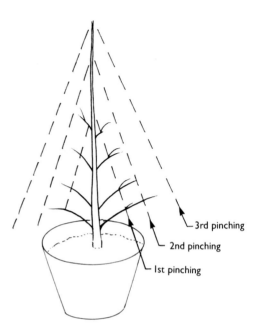

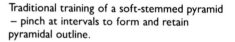

Traditional training of a soft-stemmed pyramid – pinch at intervals to form and retain pyramidal outline.

into 5in (13cm) pots. Stake each plant separately, and tie in the stem every 2–3in (5–8cm). Keep the plants growing steadily through winter at 58°F (14°C) minimum. Mist over on fine days, and pick off any flower buds which form, to conserve plant energy. During the spring, pot on into 8–10in (20–25cm) containers, before the roots have had a chance to become matted and pot-bound. When you are growing smaller pyramids, adjust the size of pot accordingly. Continue to tie in to the stake and start liquid feeding as for standards. Mist over plants regularly and shade them from strong sun. As the side-shoots develop, train them out near to the horizontal, but at a slight *upward* angle. Those at the base should be tied on to carnation-type rings attached to the central cane.

Pinching

After stopping the main stem at 4–5ft (1.2–1.5m) – or at whatever height you require – the development of side-shoots accelerates, and serious pinching has to begin. Pinching serves a dual role – firstly, it thickens up the foliage and produces a bushy effect, and secondly it shapes up the pyramid. When shaping a pyramid, pinch the side-shoots at the top closer to the main stem than those at or near the base, with an even gradation in between. It is not unknown for the side-shoots near the base to need pinching two or three times before the topmost side-shoots are pinched once. The pyramid is now ready for routine care.

Multi-stemmed Pyramids

A variation on the pyramid theme is the multi-stem pyramid or 'wigwam', often seen at major flower shows, but little tried by amateurs. This is a pity because multi-stem pyramids are relatively easy to train, and they always make an excellent focal point in the home or plant room, or as a summer feature on a sheltered patio. The choice of plant is all-important. 'Creeping Charlie' (*Ficus pumila*) is a good candidate for this purpose. The most economic way to make a start is to buy in one decent bushy plant and cannibalise it by taking cuttings.

Calculate on five young plants being needed to make up a 6in (15cm) pot display, and up to eight for an 8in (20cm), but always allow a few extra for losses. Root the cuttings during July or August in warmth, placing no more than about six around the edge of a 3½in (9cm) pot. When rooted, in 3–4 weeks, pot up two per 3in (8cm) pot. Stake and tie, using one split cane for each plant. The growth of the main stem is usually faster and less lop-sided when it is supported and trained upwards,

than when it is left to ramble. To ensure quick growth, aim to provide the best possible growing conditions. Well-lit surroundings and the avoidance of heavy shade and overcrowding will help, and you should maintain a minimum temperature of 50°F (10°C) during winter.

Grow the plants on until the roots start to encircle the outsides of the rootball – they are then ready to pot on into their final display container. Make the move preferably in late winter or spring, and set the plants round the edges of the container. As with traditional pyramids, training is a two-part operation – frame building followed by filling out. Again, it is best to train and grow plants indoors.

Frame Building

First, erect suitable supports. Push a bamboo cane or metal stake vertically into the centre of the pot – a 3ft (90cm) cane for a 6in (15cm)

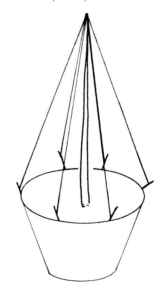

For a multi-stemmed pyramid, train 6–8 plants up wire or string supports attached to central cane.

pot, or a 5ft (1.5m) cane for a 8in (20cm) container would be about right. Next, push a peg into the compost beside each plant. Fasten a length of string or plastic-coated wire neatly from each peg to the top of the central cane, maypole fashion. Train the central main stem of each plant up its appropriate wire and tie in at 2in (5cm) intervals, taking care not to strangle the stems by tying too tightly. To improve the growth rate, shorten all side-shoots back to about three leaves, and continue to do so until each main stem reaches the top of its cane. At this point, stop the main stems by taking out the growing points. Continue to provide the best possible growing conditions – ventilate in hot weather and shade from strong sun.

Filling Out

Pinch out all new side-shoots at three to five leaves to encourage bushiness and thickening up of the foliage. Once it is fairly dense, routine maintenance can start.

Annual Cordons

Where the growth habit is naturally climbing or trailing, ornamental plants, as well as various food crops, can be trained cordon fashion. The chief merits of cordon culture are high quality, together with a longer, more sustained period of flowering and cropping. Ornamentals which are particularly well suited to cordon culture are sweet peas, ipomoea and decorative runner beans.

As with other forms of pinch and prune sculpture, the best results are obtained where a high standard of plant care prevails, and this includes good soil management. Annual cordons are grown successfully both *in situ*, in beds or borders, and in containers. Where they are grown *in situ*, thorough soil preparation is of the utmost importance.

The training of annual cordons starts early in life. Sow these half-hardy annuals indoors, either singly in small pots, or thinly and then pricked out singly into 3–3½in (8–9cm) pots. Keep plants growing steadily at all times, and harden off any plant thoroughly before setting it outdoors. Select suitable, warm, sheltered positions when you are planting or standing out.

Supports

There are three distinct stages in the training of annual cordons, and the first of these is the provision of adequate supports. A handy form of support for ornamental sweet peas, ipomoea, and runner beans is the 'wigwam' (*see* page 69), with a neat but more substantial central support of up to 7ft (2m) in height. Another alternative is to use one individual 6–8ft (1.8–2.4m) cane per plant. The quickest and easiest way to attach the plant to its support is to use pea rings every 3in (8cm) – this is very reliable.

Frame Building

This is the second stage. For best results with sweet peas, you should pinch out the growing point at the third leaf, and train up the strongest shoot as the main stem. When cordon sweet peas reach the top of their supports, they are dropped down and systematically trained up another conveniently positioned support (*see* diagram). Runner beans and ipomoea are allowed to run freely to the top of their supports before having their growing points removed. Unlike sweet peas, they need no tying.

Stopping and Side-Shooting

In the case of sweet peas, you need to remove the tendrils as well as the side-shoots, as soon

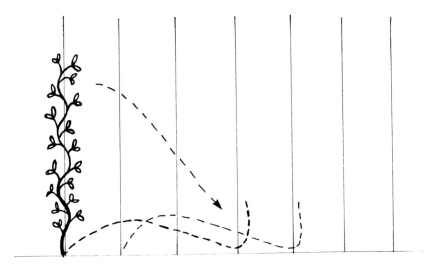

For cordon sweet peas, untie the plants when they reach the tops of their supports, gently lower the stem to the ground, and then train up a new support.

as they are big enough to handle. This is a job for alternate days. With runners and ipomoea, pinch out the tips of side-shoots at the third leaf, and of the secondary side-shoots at one leaf.

ROUTINE MAINTENANCE OF SOFT-STEMMED SCULPTURES

Your prime aims should be to keep plants healthy and in good shape as well as to enhance and retain their decorative effect. This means no let-up in looking after them, especially in matters such as feeding, watering, dead-heading and picking over dead and yellowing leaves.

Traditional Standards

Continue to pinch out the tips of side-shoots as soon as they make 2–3in (5–8cm) of growth. This is especially important if you find

that the plants are not branching and thickening up naturally. In autumn annual standards, such as coleus, are discarded, and with geraniums and fuchsias the youngest and softest side-shoots are cut back to within a leaf of the older stems. In spring, when growth recommences, you can resume the pinching of side-shoots. Discard old plants when stems and growth becomes hard and flowering tails off.

You can expect the useful life of a geranium standard to be about 3 years, of a fuchsia 5 years, and marmalade plant and lantana up to 7 years. Make allowances for this and your planning ahead and start off new replacement standards in plenty of time.

Multi-stem Standards

Routine maintenance here is largely a matter of shortening the trails which cascade down the sides to 6in (15cm), and of thinning out overcrowded side-shoots. Also important is

71

the prompt removal of damaged or diseased growth.

Traditional Pyramids

Once the initial framework is formed, the subsequent treatment of traditional pyramids closely follows that of traditional standards. Short-lived coleus and perilla pyramids are discarded in the autumn.

Multi-stem Pyramids

The aim here is to keep plants growing steadily. Carry on with occasional pinching to maintain plenty of foliage. Cut out old side-shoots, both at the base of plants and higher up, and tie in handy replacement growths. If you do this on a rota basis, the useful life of the pyramid will be greatly prolonged.

Discard plants when they are past their best – this is usually within 5 to 7 years for a smaller plant in a 6in (15cm) pot. Those in upwards of 8in (20cm) containers may flourish for 10–15 years or more, provided renewal of old side-shoots takes place systematically. Regular repotting in alternate years with topdressing in the interim should take place as a matter of routine.

Annual Cordons

Keep up the rounds of pinching and side-shooting. To ensure a continuation of flowering, dead-heading is also a must. All annuals are discarded in the autumn.

TRAINING WOODY-STEMMED SCULPTURES

As most woody-stemmed plant sculptures are grown and trained outdoors, careful siting is essential, being important, not only from a garden design viewpoint, but also from the angle of the plant's health. Unlike indoor growing, outdoor cultivation is subject to the vagaries of climate and weather over which the gardener has no control. Good growing conditions, plus fertile soil and composts, are of high priority as a back-up to training if you want a satisfactory end result.

As with all pinch and prune sculptures, it is vital to start with suitable varieties. See the plant reference section for details on plants for special purposes.

Free-standing Sculptures – Traditional Standards

Many plants which are normally grown as shrubs, including azaleas, buddleia, hibiscus, broom, lilac and rose, are suitable to train successfully as standards, and most trees can be trained in a similar way. Traditional standards are normally trained to provide a clear length of main stem, varying from about 3½ft (1m) up to 7ft (2m). In gardening circles, those with 3–5ft (1–1.5m) clear stem are often referred to as short or half standards, while those over 5ft (1.5m) are described as full standards. As with topiary standards, training is a two-part operation – stem building followed by crown formation.

Stem Building

As one of the first requirements is a strong, sturdy, main stem, many trees and shrubs need to be budded or grafted on to suitable rootstocks before training can begin. This is often because the ideal garden variety is incapable of producing a strong enough trunk on its own roots. In other cases, it will not grow tall enough to give a sufficient length of clear stem.

There are often problems with home budding and grafting, and a useful compromise may be to buy in whips or lining-out stock suitably budded or grafted. These are young plants which have not been pruned, and consist of a single, whippy, unbranched main stem. Deciduous tree and shrub whips are normally bought in and planted out or potted up during autumn. Evergreens are ideally dealt with in spring (but autumn makes a good second best). Given a suitable, warm, sheltered spot and fertile soil, direct-planted hardy stock represent less work than container-grown plants. Plant out or pot up at the same depth as before the move.

You will need to nurse the young stock along – stake, tie, water and feed as for topiary standards. Allow the main stem to reach the required height of clear stem, plus 6–8in (15–20cm) to allow for crown formation (see below). This may take a couple of years or more in the case of slow-growing trees and shrubs. In the mean time, side-shoots which develop up the stems should be pinched out at the three-leaf stage during the summer months. Pinch out subsequent secondary side-shoots at one leaf.

Crown Formation

With traditional standards the aim is to form a framework of four to five main branches, so when the main stem has produced a minimum of six leaves or buds above clear stem height, remove the growing point. Ideally, you should stop evergreens in late spring or summer. Autumn is the best time for deciduous trees and shrubs, as there is less risk of weakening the plant. Allow the subsequent new main shoots to put on a full season's growth, and, during this time, remove the side-shoot stubs to clean up the main stem. Deal with evergreens in the summer and deciduous types in the autumn.

The following year, cut out weak and spindly shoots, leaving four or five of the strongest and best to form the initial main framework. Shorten them back by a third to a half, and then allow each of them to grow on and branch out. Treat them as before, but this time only leave two or three of the strongest shoots. At this stage, revert to routine pinch and prune treatment suited to the individual tree or shrub.

Miniature Standards

These are treated in much the same way as traditional standards, but on a reduced time and size scale. They are usually container-grown, and rarely planted direct.

Stem Building

A 6–18in (15–45cm) clear stem is about right. It is normally achieved in a season and often without the need to use budded or grafted stock.

Crown Formation

This varies slightly in that the main branches are pruned when they reach the required length. You do not need to wait for a full season's growth.

Weeping Standards

The training of weeping standards provides a classic example of the need for budded or grafted stock. Because of the naturally prostrate or weeping nature of these plants, a stem builder, in the form of a suitable rootstock, is necessary before the required stem height can be achieved. Commercially this is done by budding and grafting high up, and this is known as 'top worked stock' in gardening jargon. Those intent on budding and grafting at home should bear this in mind. In the case of some weeping standards, such as roses, willow and

73

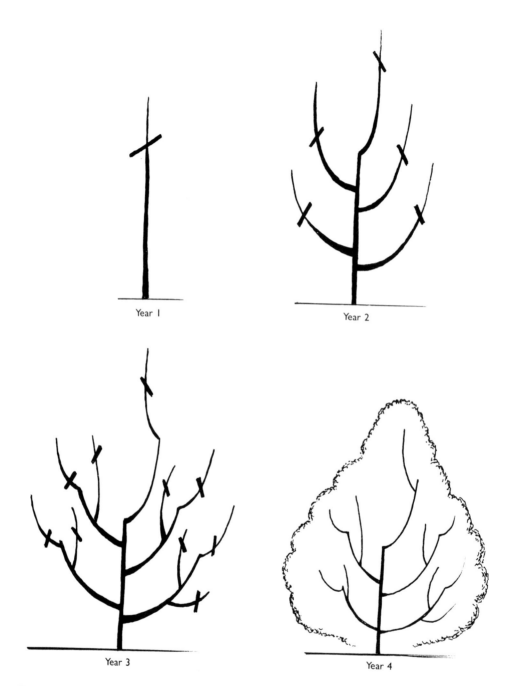

Year 1

Year 2

Year 3

Year 4

Traditional training of a hard-stemmed pyramid – formation pruning
takes place in years 1, 2, and 3, and then summer pruning in year 4 and
subsequently.

purple beech, it is best to opt for a clear stem height of up to 10ft (3m). This is to allow sufficient headroom for the weeping branches to be displayed to optimum advantage.

Crown formation broadly follows the treatment outlined for traditional standards. Shorten back new shoots by a third to a half for a couple of seasons before reverting to routine pruning.

Pyramids

Broadly speaking, there are two main ways of training hardy trees and shrubs into the traditional pyramid shape, and your choice of method should be largely dictated by the inherent natural habit of the plant in question. First is the assisted natural shaping approach. This amounts to nothing more than giving a tree or shrub a helping hand to exploit its own natural pyramidal tendency. It involves simply shortening back or cutting out long, straggly or misplaced shoots which distract the eye from the pyramidal outlines.

The second technique is suitable for training trees of varying natural habit into the pyramidal form. It relies on pinching and pruning and is a two-part operation.

Frame Building

The aim when training a traditional standard is to create a framework of branches on top of a 12in (30cm) short leg, or main trunk. After planting out a young tree or shrub cut it back by one-third, then allow it to make a full season's growth, giving every care and encouragement to promote a vigorous root system. By the end of the first season the plants should have produced several new shoots. Ideally, there will be a strong central leader at the top, plus three or four vigorous growths lower down, with maybe a few weaker ones as well. Pruning at this stage

involves cutting out the weakest growths back to one leaf or bud (deciduous in autumn, evergreens in late spring). Next, deal with the main leader, and the three or four vigorous shoots which have been left behind after culling out the weak growths. Shorten them by one-third if good growth has been made, or by a half if stronger future vigour is required.

At the end of the second growing season a new leader should have developed, along with another three or four new vigourous shoots. Treat these as in the previous year, cutting out weak growths and shortening back. In addition, shorten back by one-third the new growth which has been made on the previous year's vigorous shoots. Continue shortening back each new season's leader and vigorous growths in the same way, until the pyramid has reached an optimum size in keeping with its setting.

Shaping

Summer prune the new season's side-shoots back to three or four leaves during the period from June to August. If vigour is lacking with deciduous varieties, defer summer pruning until the autumn, then shorten back the side-shoots by a half to two-thirds.

When pruning or pinching you should never stick slavishly to any rule of thumb if it is likely to ruin the tree or shrub outline. This should always be of high priority, and you should be aiming for a broad-based sculpture with a tapered top.

Once the size and shape meet with approval, revert to routine maintenance.

Spindle Bush

Apart from its use in commercial fruit growing, the spindle bush does not seem to have caught on in Britain. This is difficult to

75

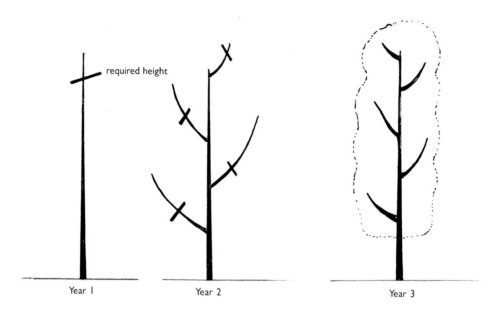

Year 1   Year 2   Year 3

When training a spindle bush, you should prune in years 1 and 2 as shown, and then revert to normal summer pruning in year 3 and subsequently.

understand since it is fairly popular and widespread on the Continent. As the name implies, a spindle bush consists in essence of a vertical, single spindle or axis, around which shoots and branches grow. From the decorative point of view the effect is of a vertical column, and it is a useful form for framing views, entrances, steps and so on.

Training a spindle bush is not normally very different from shaping a single cordon. Conventionally, young whips are planted out, staked individually, and tied in at 2in (5cm) intervals. The central stem is allowed to develop naturally, and the main leader is stopped once the bush has reached the desired ultimate height. Side-shoots of the current season's growth, which arise up the main stems, are summer pruned back to the third leaf in July or August.

Routine maintenance takes over once this stage is reached.

Festoon

This is a new method of training and restraining vigorous, strong-growing deciduous trees, such as plum and cherry, in small gardens, creating what is, in effect, an enforced weeping form of sculpture. Festooning is highly successful with fruit trees, and shows considerable promise with decorative varieties as well. Success depends on the restraining effect of bending down branches, and the resulting free-flowering response.

The aim is to train trees as bushes on 12–24in (30–60cm) stems. To achieve this, young whips are cut back at between 18–30in (45–75cm), and resultant growths are summer pruned in July or August, when they are shortened back by one-third. They are then bent over and downwards and tied to pegs to pull them below the horizontal. When the process is repeated in the second year,

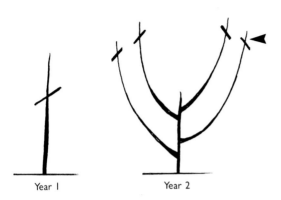

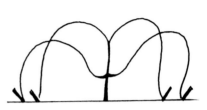

Year 1   Year 2

To train a festoon form, cut in years 1 and 2 as shown, then tie down the branches after pruning in year 2. Revert to summer pruning in subsequent years.

the main frame should be complete. Subsequently, new growths are summer pruned back to five leaves, and then routine maintenance takes over.

Bonsai

The training of Bonsai trees follows a basically similar pattern to that of other woody-stemmed sculptures – frame building followed by shaping. However, with Bonsai there is the additional complication of root pruning. In fact, the pruning and training of Bonsai from the purist viewpoint is a highly developed and complex business – a book subject on its own – and serious Bonsai enthusiasts are referred to specialist works for the finer points and differing styles. Bonsai is a fascinating, but slow and time-consuming occupation, hence the high cost of trained or part-trained trees – running into hundreds of pounds in extreme cases. The following notes are aimed at the amateur of limited means who wishes to dabble and gain experience in Bonsai.

For the first tree, you should not attempt anything too ambitious. Stick to simple, straightforward shapes such as the single upright or leaning tree. Windswept semi-cascade and cascade shapes are best reserved until you have gained a modicum of experience.

Frame Building

Ideally, you should start with a young (two to five-year-old) tree of a suitable variety – use seedlings, rooted cuttings or bought-in grafted stock. Pot in the spring, reducing the rootball size by one-third to a half, and prune the top with the aim of creating a spiral arrangement of three to five (or more) main branches. Cut out badly placed and weak shoots, and shorten back the main shoots by a half to two-thirds.

Shaping

This is a continuous and ongoing process throughout the spring and the summer. Allow young shoots to make ½–¾in (1–2cm) of new growth and then shorten back to within ¼in (6mm) of old wood.

Routine Maintenance

This will be a continuation of shaping, pinching and pruning. Whenever you are potting or repotting the plant, reduce the rootball size by up to a quarter.

Wall-trained Sculptures

The growing and training of wall plant sculptures is a long-established art and craft which is normally associated more with fruit growing than with purely decorative effects. My emphasis here is on the latter. Most recognised forms of wall sculptures are trained in two stages, involving frame building of main branches, then infilling and spur development along and between the main branches. Cordon, espalier and fan are among the most widely-used forms of sculptures which are wall-trained for decorative effect. They all fulfil the purpose of providing wall coverage and differ mainly in their varying branch patterns.

All wall-trained sculptures need supports, and horizontal straining wires with canes attached are the norm (*see* page 26).

Training Cordons

The double vertical cordon is extremely useful where the aim is to cover a tall, narrow area of wall. Avoid single and triple cordons, as they are less easy to manage than the doubles.

Frame building In the case of newly-planted or young deciduous trees and shrubs, cut back the main stem in autumn, to a good bud about 12–18in (30–45cm) above the ground. Ideally, look for another one or two healthy, plump buds just below that one good bud. Allow about three good shoots to develop, and when they are 12–18in (30–45cm) long, select the two which are best placed to make the most even pair. Train these out at 45 degrees to form a 'V' arrangement, and tie in to supports. Cut out the third shoot, shortening back any others to three

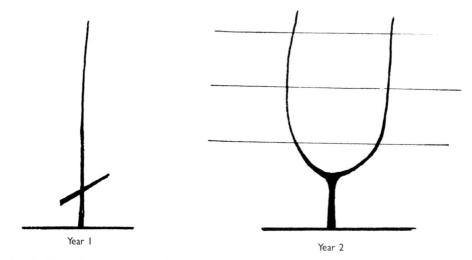

Year 1   Year 2

To train a double cordon, cut down to 12–18in (30–45cm) in year 1, and train up two arms vertically in year 2, tying in at intervals. Carry out summer pruning of side growths and leave tips uncut until required height is reached.

leaves at the same time. During late summer, before the wood has ripened, untie the twin shoots, position them vertically, spaced about 16in (40cm) apart, and re-tie.

A few evergreens can be trained as double cordons. Treat as deciduous kinds, but prune in late spring as opposed to autumn.

Shaping Once the framework of twin stems is established, shaping and keeping plants in bounds is achieved by summer pruning. This consists of shortening new summer growths back to three or four leaves, while subsequent late summer regrowths are shortened back to one leaf. Cut out promptly any shoots which grow straight into, or directly away from, the wall.

Training Espaliers

Pairs of horizontal branches, set in tiers 'fishbone' style, typify a well-developed espalier. This is a form of training which is ideal for wide expanses of wall, and the height can easily be tailored to suit the situation.

Frame building This is a slow job, and you should allow a year for each pair of branches.

Cut back the newly-planted young tree or shrub to about 2in (5cm) above the bottom horizontal wire (autumn for deciduous kinds and late spring for evergreens). Allow the three strongest shoots to grow and tie them in – one vertically and one at 45 degrees either side. In autumn, untie the two side growths, bend them down horizontally and tie in to the bottom straining wire. Then deal with the vertical leader as before, cutting it back to 2in (5cm) above the second wire. Again, cut deciduous kinds in the autumn and evergreens in the late spring. Treat the resulting three strongest shoots as before, cutting out, training out, and tying down horizontally. Continue thus, tier by tier, until the required height is attained.

Shaping and pruning In the case of ornamentals, shaping must be geared to plant habit. For instance, plants which bloom on spurs (short lengths of previous season's wood) are summer pruned in very much the same way as cordons – in other words, new growths are cut back to three or four leaves. The same guidelines apply to foliage trees and shrubs, while those plants which bloom on

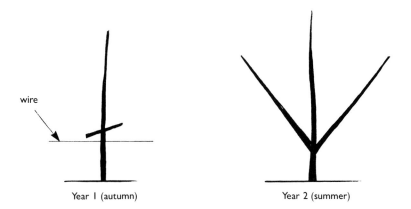

wire

Year 1 (autumn)　　　　　　　Year 2 (summer)

Training espaliers (1). In the autumn of the first year, cut down whip to 2in (5cm) above bottom wire – about 12–16in (30–40cm) above the ground. In the following summer, train up the 3 strongest shoots.

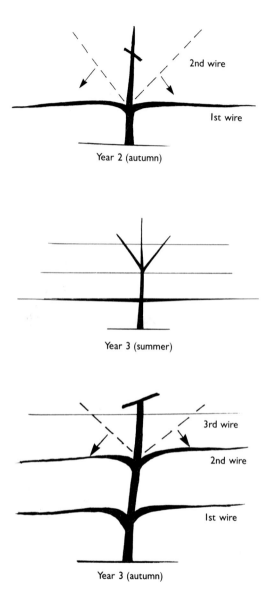

Year 2 (autumn)

Year 3 (summer)

Year 3 (autumn)

Training espaliers (II). Alternatively, tie down 2 branches horizontally in year 2, and cut the 3rd shoot 2in (5cm) above a 2nd wire. Then, in the summer of the following year, train up 3 strong shoots. In the autumn, tie down 2 arms horizontally and cut 3rd shoot just above a 3rd wire.

the tips of new season's growth should have the old flowered wood cut out in autumn or spring. *See* details on the individual plants for guidance.

Training Fans

The fan form is particularly well suited to training members of the *prunus* family, such as cherry, plum, apricot and peach. These are all ornamentals which do not take kindly to either cordon or espalier treatment. Fans are excellent for covering square areas of wall of approximately equal height and width. However, their training, frame building in particular, requires a higher degree of know-how and skill than cordon or espalier, and the subsequent shaping and routine maintenance must be more flexible. It is difficult to give a strict guide, because of the differing growth rates between topmost branches and those at the bottom. The lower branches may lack vigour while the tops are often difficult to restrain.

Frame building Begin in the spring with newly-planted *prunus* types and evergreens, and in the autumn with all other deciduous trees and shrubs. Cut out the main stem of the plant back to 2ft (60cm) from the ground (*see* diagram). During the following twelve months, train and tie in two branches at 45 degrees, 'Y' fashion, and remove all the others. With deciduous kinds, shorten the two arms of the 'Y' back to 18in (45cm) at the end of the growing season. Leave the evergreens and *prunus* until the following spring.

The following twelve months are devoted to training out four fingers, fan-wise from each of the two arms, and tying them in (*see* diagram). These are subsequently cut back to about 20in (50cm) – again, deal with the deciduous kinds in the autumn and the evergreens and *prunus* in the spring. The basic framework is then complete.

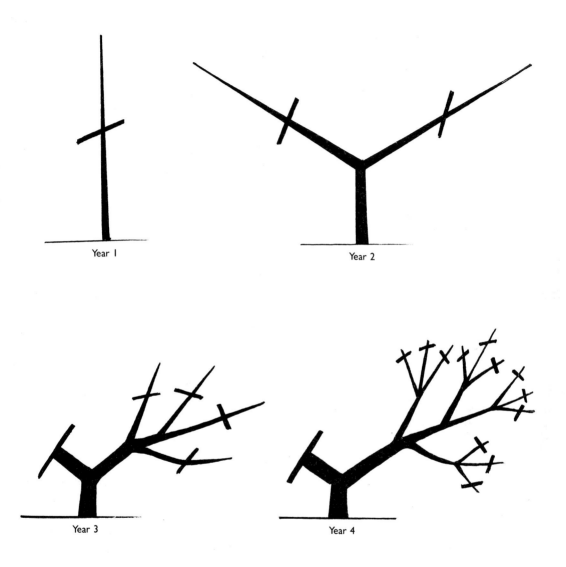

Year 1

Year 2

Year 3

Year 4

Formation pruning for training fans.

Shaping and infilling Although pinching and pruning thereafter is less exacting than for fruit growing, it can still be tricky. Basically, you should summer prune, cutting out weak side-shoots and those growing into, or away from, the wall. Shorten all the other shoots back to three or four leaves, and cut back late summer growth to one bud. However, if the top growth becomes excessive, simply tip back the topmost shoots. If the bottom growth lacks vigour, cut back hard to one or two leaves.

81

Training Wall Tracery and Treillage

These can be trained as pinch and prune wall coverings, and are ideal for anyone looking for minimal training with woody stemmed plants. Wall shrubs respond particularly well to this treatment, compared to true climbers. Suitable plant selections are nearly always limited to broad-leaved evergreens.

Frame foundation Set out young plants, and cut out weak, spindly shoots, along with any which are inward-growing or outward-facing. Aim to leave three to eight well-placed shoots. Train these to radiate out from the base and tie them in as they grow. The growing points are not cut out, except in the case of disease or damage, until the treillage reaches its allotted height.

Shaping and infilling Summer pinch and prune, shortening back side-shoots to three or four leaves.

Routine Maintenance

The subsequent routine training of established punch and prune sculptures is largely a matter of keeping the plants in good shape. This is normally a continuation of the shaping and infilling which has already been outlined under the respective individual pinch and prune forms.

REMEDIAL TREATMENT

Provided they are basically healthy, and not neglected beyond repair, there is usually some scope for renovating and rejuvenating pinch and prune sculptures. From the various ways of giving new life to ailing sculptures come two techniques which are often very successful.

Root Pruning

Sometimes newly-established trees become over-vigorous, a common shortcoming of, for example, *prunus*. Root pruning in November can curb excess vigour, and it can also make pinch and prune training easier and more effective. Dig out a semi-circular trench, about 12in (30cm) wide and of a similar depth, some 16–30in (40–75cm) out from the base of the plant. Sever all thick roots crossing the trench, disturbing the fibrous ones as little as possible, and then fill the trench with good topsoil. Repeat the process on the other side of the sculpture the following year, and be sure to stake and tie for a year or two until it is re-established.

Renewal Pruning and Training

The object of this technique is to carry through a policy of replacing old or damaged wood, without ruining the plant shape. It is a useful means of renewing the spurs or side-growths of wall-trained and intensively grown free-standing forms, such as the spindle bush. The method is fine, provided that the main branch framework is left intact. Aim to cut out old spurs on the basis of about one in four — in other words, renew old spurs on a four-year cycle. Resultant new shoots are trained in to compensate.

7 Propagation

In all forms of gardening the vexed question of whether the amateur should buy in or raise his own plants always presents itself.

BUYING IN

It is probably best to buy in slow-growing, fickle, or difficult plants, especially where there is some urgency. Buying in part-grown trees and shrubs will cut down on the necessary delay before training can begin. You can expect to wait five years – and longer with slow growers such as maple, thorn and holly – before home-raised trees are ready to plant out and train. On average, you will have to allow three years for shrubs – quick-growing *lonicera* and privet will be ready to train sooner, while slow-growing *elaeagnus* will take a lot longer. Buying in also gives you the opportunity to select the best tree or shrub for the purpose in hand. It is vital when you are creating topiary to start with a quality tree or shrub which branches well from the bottom. In the case of evergreens, the tree will need to have plenty of leaves from the base up, so that it has every chance of filling out close to the ground.

Buying in is also undoubtedly more convenient. It avoids the cost and nuisance of providing propagating facilities, and makes fewer demands on growing skills and know-how. Take the whole complex problem of rootstocks as an example. Many trees and shrubs are budded or grafted on to the roots of another closely related variety. These are commercial practices which provide you, the buyer, with the following advantages: vigour is controlled to produce trees and shrubs of a predetermined size – very often working with dwarfing stocks suited to the domestic garden; disease resistance is improved; stem building is better – this is of particular importance when you are growing plant sculptures of standard cotoneasters, standard willows and so on; varieties of trees and shrubs are propagated which cannot be raised from seed, or by other vegetative means such as the taking of cuttings. Nurserymen are specialists in the budding and grafting field and have easy access to suitable plant material. Such material is often difficult to come by when you are propagating at home.

Buying in scores where plants are long-lived and propagation is not an ongoing chore (as with, say, carpet bedding plants, chrysanthemums, geraniums, fuchsias and marguerites). In short, it makes good sense to buy in trees, shrubs, conifers and climbers – especially where budding and grafting are involved.

RAISING YOUR OWN PLANTS

Propagation can save money where a number of plants are involved, as with carpet bedding, but you must be mindful of the need to house and overwinter stock plants, which can take up a lot of room. Propagation is of enormous benefit when growing Bonsai and miniature container sculptures, as it enables a very early start to be made with training. You should propagate, too, for renovation work. Whether topiary is being used for hedging or specimen sculptures, you should keep some similar plants growing elsewhere in the garden for 'gapping up'. Take the odd cutting each year, and then dispose of older plants if space is getting short. This way, young, moveable plants will always be to hand.

Propagation can be fun, and it can give enormous satisfaction. In practice, the main activity will usually be concerned with short-lived, quick-growing plants which need frequent renewal – the half-hardy perennials.

METHODS OF PROPAGATION

Many (but not all) trees and shrubs can be raised from seed. Other methods of propagation to consider are cuttings, suckers and layers, none of which should present any problems to the keen gardener. The more complex techniques of budding and grafting are best left to professionals, as is micro-propagation – anyone determined to try their hand should study a specialist book on the subject. Some trees and shrubs are more suited to one method of propagation than another – see details on individual plants.

Generally, it takes longer to raise trees and shrubs from seed than from any other method of propagation, and it is almost inevitable that there will be some variation amongst the progeny. This is not so when trees and shrubs are raised vegetatively – by cuttings, layers, suckers, budding and grafting – when they can expect to share identical inherited characteristics with their parents. However, good and bad features can be passed on from one generation to the next, and this includes virus and other diseases. You must always propagate from healthy stock which possess desirable characteristics.

Most half-hardy perennials can be raised from seed, but (as with the trees and shrubs), not all. There is likely to be little variation amongst the resulting plants if you are using present-day seed selections from leading seed houses. Vegetative propagation is also widely used – stem and leaf cuttings, offsets, layers and division all have a place. For the best way and time to tackle the job see the individual plant details.

Growing from Seed

Always aim to use fresh seed – reputable seed houses date stamp their packets for your reference. Any seed not sown right away should be stored in a cool, dry, shaded spot at 40–45°F (4–5°C).

Preparing the Containers

Use a container with a minimum depth of 2in (5cm) and drainage holes in the base; wash and disinfect it if it has been used before. Worktops and propagators should also be kept spotlessly clean. Bottom out containers with a layer of gravel – sufficient to cover the drainage holes – and then top up with fresh, moist, proprietary seed compost. Never be tempted to re-use compost – you will run the risk of disease and failure. Soil-based composts should be firmed down at the corners and edges, using the fingers, and they should then be smoothed over with, say, the base of a jam jar, to leave a flat, even surface ½in (1cm) below the rim. Don't firm peat-based composts. It is much better to overflow the container and then remove surplus compost with a straight-edged piece of wood. Finally, tap the top gently two or three times to settle the compost.

Note Seeds of many lime-hating plants germinate poorly in composts containing lime. It is important to use lime-free seed composts and avoid watering with tap water in hard water areas. In the absence of rain water, use distilled water of the kind sold for batteries. A few other seeds are sensitive to fertiliser and germinate best in equal parts peat and sand. (See details on individual plants.)

Sowing

It is important to select the method best suited to the particular size and type of seed.

Dust-fine seed   Sprinkle clean, fine sand over the surface of the prepared container, just sufficient to enable the seed to be seen against it. Then scatter the seed thinly and evenly. It helps to use a 'V' chute of stiff paper. *Do not* cover the seed with compost. The most common cause of failure is to sow too deeply.

Small and medium seeds   Take a pinch of seed between finger and thumb and scatter evenly over the surface. Barely cover with more finely-sieved seed compost.

Large seeds   Sow 1½in (4cm) apart, or set singly into 3in (8cm) pots. Cover with sieved compost to a depth equal to the diameter of the seed and no more.

Watering and Covering

Immediately after sowing the seed, stand the container up to half its depth in a dish of clean water and leave for twenty minutes or so, by which time the surface should be visibly moist. Allow to drain and cover with a clear rigid plastic sheet, cling film or clean glass. This is to raise the level of humidity. Shade by covering over with thick paper.

Germinating

Seedlings which require no special after-treatment are kept moist and germinated within the recommended temperature range.

The majority of seeds benefit from a heated propagator and most will germinate well at 60–70°F (16–21°C). Some go 'sleepy' if temperatures rise too much for their liking, while virtually all will stand still or rot off if temperatures are too low. Turn the glass or plastic cover twice a day, wiping off condensation drips at the same time. As soon as the seedlings show signs of movement, wedge open the sheet of glass, or perforate the plastic, to allow in some air. After a few days remove the cover entirely. Grow the seedlings on at a few degrees cooler, giving them light, airy conditions and shade from direct sun. Water from below at the first suggestion of drying out, and, as soon as they are large enough to handle, prick them out. Space them out into clean trays of fresh, weak potting compost, or singly into small pots.

The majority of seeds will germinate without much trouble. However, some require special treatment if disappointments are to be avoided.

Soaking   Before seeds can germinate they must take up water, and some find this difficult. Soaking in tepid water can help, but it is important not to soak them for too long or they may suffocate through lack of air. (See details on individual plants.) Strain off surplus water before sowing.

Chipping seed coats   Some seeds have oily or hard seed coats, this restricts the uptake of water and slows down germination. Try nicking the seed case with a sharp, pointed knife. They will benefit from soaking afterwards.

Chilling   Many conifer, shrub and tree seeds germinate better if they are chilled before sowing. Either mix the seed with damp peat and store in the refrigerator for one or two months before sowing, sealed in a plastic bag.

Alternatively, sow in containers during January or February. (Be sure to cover the drainage holes in the base with fine mesh netting or gauze before filling, to stop pests crawling in through the base.) Stand outdoors in a vermin- and bird-proof place, covering with glass and an upturned box to keep out the rain. After six to eight weeks bring into the warmth to germinate.

Some tree and shrub seeds may take up to two years to germinate. These will require not one but two periods of chilling. If any tree or shrub seeds fail to germinate promptly, don't throw them out for at least 18 months, and don't allow them to dry out in the interim. Seeds requiring this double chilling are really best sown under a cold frame, with each one being pricked out as soon as it appears.

Vegetative Propagation

Soft and Semi-Ripe Cuttings

Be careful to take cuttings from shoots which are not carrying flower buds or flowers, and never take cuttings from a plant showing signs of wilting – water generously the day before-hand. It is wise to take cuttings in the cool of the early part of the day, when they are most likely to be fully charged with water, and you should use a sharp knife or secateurs to 'take' the cuttings, and a sharp razor blade to 'trim' them. Drop the cuttings into a plastic bag as they are taken, and close it. This is to avoid unnecessary wilting to which softwood cuttings are especially prone.

Prepare pots of proprietary cutting com-post *before* taking the cuttings. This will reduce to a minimum the time lost before taking cuttings and potting them.

Softwood cuttings are susceptible to rotting (as are semi-hardwood, but to a lesser degree). As a preventive, dip prepared cuttings into fungicide – some gardeners prefer to use proprietary rooting prepara-tions, but these can be a mixed blessing. The milky, sappy *echeveria* and *sedum* benefit from being dipped into charcoal.

Dibble cuttings to no more than a third their length around the edges of a small pot – a pencil is useful for this purpose. Never bury the leaves or you run risk of them rotting.

Until the roots have formed, more moisture is lost through the leaves than is absorbed through the base. While the cuttings are still rooting, you can minimise this loss by encasing the entire pot in an inflated, clear plastic bag, sealed at the top with an elastic band. Open the bag each day to get rid of stale air, and spray the cuttings regularly with tepid water.

All cuttings should be rooted in daylight but need to be shaded from direct sun.

Softwood cuttings Used for half-hardy herbaceous perennials – cuttings are taken from early spring to summer (*see* details on individual plants).

Cut off a soft young shoot, avoiding those which are thick, sappy, hollow, weak or spindly. Each cutting should be from 1–3in (3–8cm) in length and must include a minimum of two leaf joints. Trim them cleanly and squarely, just below the bottom leaf joint, and strip away the lower pair of leaves before inserting in cutting compost.

Place the pots of cuttings (encased in plastic bags) on a warm window-sill, shaded from strong sun. Better still, use a propagator or seed tray soil warmer where the bottom heat will speed the process up. Expect rooting in about three weeks. The cuttings will become turgid when they have rooted, and at this stage you should open up the top of the bag to allow air to circulate and prevent too sudden a drop in humidity. Drop the temperature slightly and remove the plastic bag after four days, standing the pots on moist, pebble-filled saucers. After a further week to ten days, pot up singly into 3in (8cm) pots of potting compost and grow on.

Semi-ripe wood cuttings Used for evergreen and deciduous trees, shrubs and climbers. Cuttings are taken in midsummer as soon as the young growths have partially ripened and begun to harden.

The way semi-ripe cuttings are treated is varied to suit individual plants. After trimming, you should aim for a cutting of 4–6in (10–15cm) in length somewhat longer than with softwoods.

With the *traditional method*, select terminal shoots and cut well into the ripened hardwood, making sure each cutting has at least two leaf joints. Trim the base as for a softwood cutting, and then cut out the soft tip, just above the top pair of leaves. Pull off the lower leaves to expose about a third of the stem.

Heel cuttings give a higher success rate with some plants. Pull a side-shoot gently downwards and away from the main stem, so that a sliver of older stem comes away with it. Trim off any ragged edges from this 'heel', and remove tip and lower leaves as described for the traditional cutting.

Internode cuttings are useful for clematis, ivy and Virginia creeper for convenience and ease of rooting. Take cuttings as before. Trim the bottom 2in (5cm) or so below a leaf joint. Trim at the top just above the same leaf joint, so leaving a single leaf or pair of leaves. Insert the cutting up to the base of the leaf or leaves.

The hardiest semi-ripe wood cuttings will root under a shaded closed frame or cloche. However, most do best given the bottom heat of a propagator or soil warmer, or on a warm window-sill encased in plastic bags. Expect rooting in about a month to six weeks.

Hardwood Cuttings

This method is in the main for deciduous shrubs, and for a few trees. Cuttings are taken in autumn, just as the leaves fall, when the wood is hard and there is still enough warmth

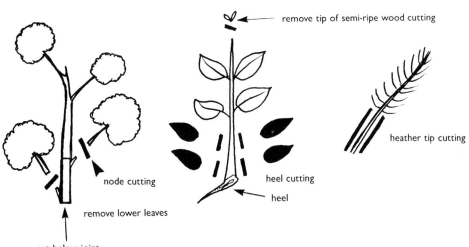

remove tip of semi-ripe wood cutting

node cutting

heel cutting

heel

heather tip cutting

remove lower leaves

cut below joint

Preparing softwood cuttings and semi-ripe wood cuttings.

in the soil to give the cuttings a good start. (There are exceptions – see individual plant details.) Lavender, for example, roots best when taken in September, while *berberis* can be taken any time up to December.

Cuttings are rooted in a sheltered spot outdoors, protected from north and east winds, or under frames or cloches. Prepare dibber holes about 7in (18cm) deep by trickling 1in (3cm) of sand into the bottom.

Use vigorous stems which have just completed their first year's growth. Select well-ripened, pencil-thick, firm shoots of about 12–16in (30–40cm) in length – this allows for trimming. A prepared cutting of about 8–12in (20–30cm) is about right. Cut them out near to the joint with the main stem, and trim the bottom squarely just below a leaf joint. Cut out the soft tip about 1/8in (3mm) above a bud and right back into hard wood. Drop into the prepared dibber hole, firming well to make sure the prepared cutting is in close contact with the sand.

Re-firm cuttings if they are lifted by frost or the wind, and keep them watered and weed-free. Expect them to be rooted and ready to move by the following autumn – slower rooting kinds are best left undisturbed for another year. If cuttings are rooted under frames or cloches, ventilate freely on mild days until spring when covers must be left off.

Leaf Cuttings

Used for half-hardy, fleshy-leaved perennials, such as *echeveria* and *sedum*. Cuttings are best taken in spring or early summer.

Detach a healthy, mature leaf when it is almost full size. Place it on newspaper in cool shade for about four hours to part-dry, then treat the wounded surface where it broke away from the parent plant as for stem cuttings, by dipping first in fungicide then in charcoal. Insert the leaf upright at the edge of a small pot of cutting compost so that at least two-thirds of the blade is clear of the compost. Subsequently, treat as for the soft stem cuttings, but omit the daily damping over. Roots and shoots will develop from the base of the leaf blade.

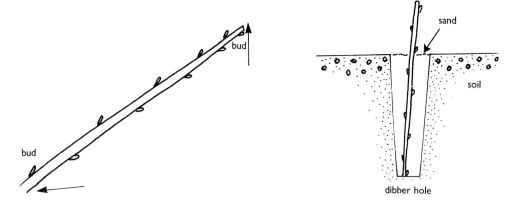

Preparing hardwood cuttings – cut below bud at bottom end, and above bud at top end. Insert cutting in sand-lined dibber hole and firm in, with one-third above the ground and two-thirds buried.

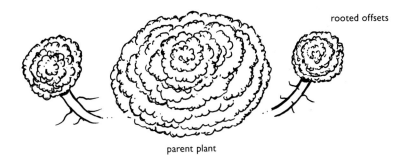

rooted offsets

parent plant

To make use of offsets, detach and pot up.

Offsets

Used for plants such as *echeveria*, and some *sedum*, which readily produce young plants alongside the parent, quickly overcrowding the container. Summer is a good time to deal with offsets.

Although offsets can be cut away with a knife, it is often better to knock plants out of their containers, loosen up the roots, tease away the old compost and pull the rooted offsets clear. Pot them up without delay and re-pot the parent plant too.

Division

Used for clump-forming, half-hardy perennials, not only as a means of increase, but also to rejuvenate plants. Healthy plants should remain in good condition indefinitely if they are split up regularly – say, every four years or so. Division is carried out when plants are resting. This is usually at any time from October to March, and ideally just before growth starts in spring.

Simply knock plants out of their containers, poke the compost out from amongst the roots, and then pull the plants apart by hand, splitting them up into several smaller ones.

Make sure each portion has some healthy roots and strong buds. Dust any wounded surfaces with a fungicide such as flowers of sulphur. Re-pot into fresh compost promptly – they must not be allowed to dry out. Ruthlessly dispose of the worn-out centre portions of old plants.

Layering

Used in the main for climbing, trailing, spreading or bushy perennial plants. Layering can be successfully carried out at any time between March and November, but you should avoid the height of summer. Soft-stemmed plants are best layered in spring.

Select a strong one or two-year-old shoot. Remove the leaves to expose a 6in (15cm) length of clear stem, about 12in (30cm) back from the tip. Next, take a sharp knife, and, at the point where the leaves were removed, make a slanting cut, about half-way through the stem from the underside. Alternatively, twist the stem to break the surface. Scoop out a shallow hollow at the point where the wounded stem meets the ground, and pin the stem down firmly into it – a wooden peg or stiff wire works well. To encourage upward growth, bend the tip up and tie to a short

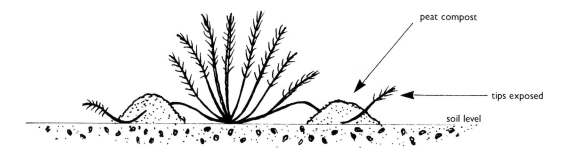

peat compost

tips exposed

soil level

Layering heathers – peg down the long young growths of heathers, using wires, and cover with peat compost, leaving the tips exposed.

bamboo cane pushed down firmly into the ground. Finally, pack around the wounded area of stem with weak potting compost. Alternatively, pin the layers down into sunken pots of weak potting compost. Omit the cutting or twisting with soft-stemmed plants such as *clematis* and *glechoma* – these should be simply pegged down into pots of moist compost.

Keep the soil moist around the layer. As soon as it is well rooted (it usually takes a year or two with woody plants and about six months with soft-stemmed), sever it from the parent plant. Leave undisturbed for a further fortnight or so, then lift and pot up.

GROWING ON AND HARDENING OFF

Newly Pricked-out Seedlings

Gradually drop the temperature down by 10°F (6°C) over a period of ten days to a fortnight. Take similar action with newly potted-up, propagator-rooted cuttings.

Hardening off in Spring

Harden off all indoor-raised plants throughout before moving them indoors. If you have frames, you can move plants out under these in the spring. Give them a little ventilation on the first few days, and increase this gradually until eventually the frame covers can be left off overnight. Allow at least another couple of days before moving the plants out of the frame. Fine mesh netting secured over an open frame will keep off birds, and at the same time provide shade and increased humidity during the day and give protection at night. You will find this a useful piece of equipment for hardening off. When you are using cloches for hardening off, make sure the ends are sealed to avoid a 'wind tunnel effect'. Although frames and cloches make hardening off easier, they are not essential. Stand plants outdoors in a sheltered spot, shaded from direct sun, for a few hours each day, as long as the weather is fine. Initially it helps to stand them in boxes which are deep enough to give protection around the sides. Give longer daily airings until the plants can eventually be left out all night.

Hardening off Semi-ripe Cuttings

Semi-ripe cuttings, rooted under a frame, or a cloche or in a propagator during July, also need hardening off. Give them increased ventilation to ripen the wood and so increase winter hardiness. These cuttings need to be kept under cover during their first winter, and hardened off completely in spring before being set outdoors for the summer.

Hardened-off half-hardy perennials are ready for decorative use as soon as all danger of frost has past. Standards in the process of being trained are stood outside in a warm sheltered spot for the summer. Young trees and shrubs are potted on progressively into larger containers and overwintered for the first two years until ready for training.

EQUIPMENT AND SUNDRIES FOR PROPAGATION

Tools

- Knife and razor blades
- Pruners
- Dibbers – pencil-thick for pricking out; 1in (3cm) for planting out hardwood cuttings
- Firmer – a clean jam jar will do perfectly well
- Sieve
- Mister
- Watering-can and rose

Equipment and Facilities

- Heated propagator or soil seed tray warmer with cover
- Garden frame or cloches
- Greenhouse for the real enthusiast

Sundries

- Seed trays plus glass or plastic covers, or cling film
- Assortment of pots
- Chemicals such as rooting hormones, insecticides, fungicides and slug bait
- Seed, and potting or multi-purpose composts

8 Plant Health

With any plant sculpture, appearance is all-important, and good-looking plants are usually healthy plants. To a large extent, therefore, success in creating topiary depends on keeping plants free of any ailments. It is vital to give top priority to preventive measures, and to resort to remedial treatment the moment trouble strikes. In practice, the most important preventive measure is to select in the first instance those trees and plants which will suit the garden, and then to follow up this careful selection with good cultivation as the first line of defence. A vigorous, well-grown plant is less likely to succumb to disease, and is better able to shake off pest attack, than a weaker one. It will also recover better from any set-back.

DIAGNOSIS

Failure to pinpoint the true cause of any problem can result in the wrong treatment.

The trouble can continue unchecked and the plants will be ruined — a waste of time, effort and expense.

What to Look For

Keep a daily watchful eye on plants to spot the first warning signs. Plant ailments can usually be narrowed down to three main problem areas:

- Infectious, contagious diseases
- Insect and other pests
- Disorders due to unfavourable environmental conditions

Many diseases, pests and disorders have quite distinctive characteristics, which will enable them to be identified with sufficient accuracy for suitable control measures to be carried out.

PESTS

Cause	Look for
Insects	Leaves, stems, buds and roots all come under attack and are holed, chewed or eaten. On occasions leaves are blotched and mined. Grubs, caterpillars and colonies of bugs are usually to be found, as well as some evidence of distortion and stunting.
Birds	Eaten or shredded leaves. Loss of buds and fruits.
Animals	Eaten and chewed shoots and stems. Look for scratching and footprints on soft ground. A sudden browning of odd leaves, shoots or plants can be due to urination by pets or wild animals.

INFECTIOUS DISEASES

Cause	Look for	Comments
Fungi	Moulds and mildews Toadstools Rots Wilts Leaf spot Death	Spread mainly by wind- and water-borne spores. Visible outgrowths make them relatively easy to diagnose in advanced stages of disease. A reasonable degree of check is often possible with fungicides.
Bacteria	Slime Rots Wilts Gumming Death	Less common than fungi, but usually more deadly. Spread by wind and water but more likely by infected hands and knives. The bacteria gain entry mainly through wounds. Difficult to diagnose. Some can be kept in check with fungicides.
Virus	Distortion Leaf mottle Colour breaking Stunted growth	Carried mainly in plant sap, and spread by sap-sucking insects and by infected sap on hands and knives, as well as by propagating from infected plants. No cure or control. Grub out and dispose of plants out of harm's way.

DISORDERS

Cause	Look for
Nutritional	Small pale leaves, interveinal yellowing, reddening or purpling of leaf margins, poor growth or excessive growth.
Weather and environment	Browned foliage due to wind scorch, sunburn or frost injury. Heavy snow falls can force sculptures out of shape and break off branches. Hail damage, cold winter die-back with blackening of shoot tips. Wilting in drought.
Incorrect cultivations	Weak, spindly growth and bare stems due to overcrowding and excess shade. Untidiness due to neglect. Death or stunting due to poor soil conditions, root damage or competition from weeds.

What to do

One very successful approach is to back up sound cultural measures with the discriminative use of chemicals.

Cultural Measures

- Practise strict hygiene
- Ensure good cultivations and give timely attention to detail when feeding, watering, pruning and providing shelter
- Make good use of traps and scarers where appropriate

Chemical Measures

Where there is a history of a particular problem, the preventive application of chemicals as a matter of routine is justified. Don't wait for problems to get a hold where there is obviously a very real risk of them doing so. Apply a suitable chemical at the first suspicion of trouble.

- Always follow the maker's instructions
- Don't use chemicals when rain is forecast, or during rainfall or much of the effect will be lost
- Don't use them in strong sun or drought — you will risk scorch
- Never use them in frosty weather when irreparable damage could be done
- Opt for approved chemicals which have been cleared for safety. They will always carry a large letter 'A' on the container

DISEASES

	Symptoms	Treatment
Bacterial canker	Attacks bark. Small circular or oval patches surrounded by raised, roughened bark are typical. The sunken centres often rot. Infection is through pruning wounds and stubs, insect injury, or diseased tissue. If cankers are allowed to encircle a branch it will die. Cherry and plum are mainly at risk.	Remove cankers promptly. With small cankers, cut out the affected area and smooth over with a sharp knife. Paint over immediately with proprietary anti-canker compound. Where a branch is completely encircled remove it.
Foot and root rots	Roots decay and discolour. Leaves wither and yellow, with death of the plant as the disease progresses. The plants most at risk are the half-hardy perennials, especially geraniums and *alternanthera*.	Remove badly-infected plants and treat the remainder by soil drenching with fungicide.
Grey mould	Stem, leaves and flowers suffer. The infected tissue first softens up, then decays and blackens with an outgrowth of grey, fluffy mould. Plants most at risk are the leafy, half-hardy herbaceous perennials.	Hand pick diseased leaves and flowers, and cut out badly affected stems. Then spray with fungicide. Try to improve air circulation.

DISEASES

	Symptoms	Treatment
Honey fungus	Trees and shrubs progressively wilt and die. Honey-coloured toadstools appear at or near ground level. The disease is spread mainly by blackish-brown bootlace-like strands travelling out from the tree underground, but also by wind-borne spores. Most trees and shrubs are at risk but especially privet and conifers.	Dig out diseased trees and shrubs, along with the bootlace-like strands. Drench the surrounding ground with proprietary honey fungus fungicide to try to contain the spread, and clean up the land prior to replanting.
Mildews	Whitish, bluish or oatmeal dusts and powders coat leaves, shoot-tips, buds and flowers. They disfigure and weaken the plant. Plants most susceptible include thorn, crab, pear, rose, vine, and chrysanthemum.	On woody plants, cut out badly-affected shoots. Apply fungicide at the first signs of attack and repeat throughout the growing season. After a severe attack, spray shrubs and trees as a matter of routine in succeeding years.
Replant disease (soil sickness)	Plants fail to get established in new positions, become unthrifty, and die. All plants are at risk.	When gapping up, dig out the old soil and dispose of it, then replant in fresh soil. Practice rotation with the half-hardy perennials.
Thuja blight	Burning, scorched and blackened foliage gets a hold on the shaded side and spreads progressively. The *thuja* family are at risk.	Cut out diseased shoots and spray repeatedly with fungicide. Thin out surrounding plants to improve air circulation.
Wilts	Growth is stunted and the leaves flag. The half-hardy perennials are vulnerable.	If dry, try watering; if over-wet, try drying the plants out a bit. Either way, if they don't recover, grub them out.
Damping off	Typically seedlings rot off at soil level, fall over and die. This is due to infection by any one of a number of disease organisms. All seedlings are at risk.	There is no cure — prevention is the only means of control. Sow seeds in clean containers and use fresh compost. Treat the newly-sown seeds with fungicide where there has been trouble in the past. Avoid over-watering, stagnant cold or very warm conditions.

DISORDERS

	Symptoms	Treatment
Bare stems	Loss of foliage at the base due to overcrowding, shade or urination by pets.	Where practical, train nearby shoots or branches to cover up gaps. Reduce shade.
Chlorosis	Unthrifty plants with yellowing leaves. The most common causes are attempting to grow acid-loving trees and shrubs in soil with a high level of chalk or lime, or watering container-grown specimens with hard mains water.	If the soil is chalky or overlies limestone, grow acid-lovers in containers of lime-free compost. The recognised control of chlorosis is to drench with iron sequestrene, but this is expensive and uneconomic for all but the smallest and youngest of trees.
Foliage browning	Common causes include scorch from sun, wind or frost, or root damage due to injury, waterlogging or intolerable dryness.	Keep all newly-planted trees and shrubs well watered, and mulch generously. Spray over the foliage during hot, dry, windy weather. Use anti-wilt sprays on newly-planted conifers. Check shelter is adequate. Improve soil and avoid spray drift when using weedkiller.
Reversion	A natural phenomenon whereby a reverted green shoot grows away amongst variegated foliage.	Cut out the reverted shoot or branch before it takes over.
Leaf scorch	Leaves and shoot-tips burn and die back. Caused by sun, wind or frost.	Increase shelter with screens of netting or wattle. Don't allow frozen plants to thaw out too quickly in early morning sun — shade them. Harden off all plants thoroughly. Cover up plants before travelling long distances — never transport them on a roof rack or in an open boot.
Waterlogging	Plants become unthrifty and greyish and eventually die. Look for water sitting a long time after heavy prolonged rain.	Don't be tempted to work and puddle wet soil. Construct rubble-filled soakaways to improve drainage (see page 22).
Bud and flower drop	Buds drop before opening; flowers drop prematurely. Causes are root injury, dryness, waterlogging or draughts, violent temperature fluctuations.	Improve growing conditions generally and mulch generously.

PESTS

	Symptoms	Treatment
Aphids (blackfly and greenfly)	Colonies of greenish, bluish or blackish insects congregated around growing points. Leaves distorted, twisted and puckered. Most plants attacked.	Spray with insecticide at first signs. Following a severe attack use tar oil winter wash to destroy overwintering eggs on deciduous trees and shrubs. Dip cuttings in liquid insecticide.
Caterpillars	Leaves, buds, flowers, shoots and fruits eaten and holed. Complete defoliation under a severe attack. Caterpillars in many colours and sizes, hairy and smooth, usually stay close by. Most plants attacked.	Hand pick on a small scale. Spray with insecticide during the growing season. Use tar oil as for aphids.
Leaf miners	Wavy channels eaten out of the interior tissues of leaves, or blister-like excavations. Holly, lilac, chrysan-themums and marguerites vulnerable.	Hand pick leaves in small-scale attacks. Spray with insecticide throughout the growing season.
Scale	Small louse-like insects attach them-selves to leaf, stem or bark. They suck sap to weaken and stunt the plant. The mature insects form a hard shell to protect eggs and young. Leaves often smeared with 'honeydew' and then a growth of sooty mould. Beech, box, bay, yew, ivy and many of the half-hardy perennials suffer.	Spray with insecticide during the growing season. Where practical, in small-scale attack on Bonsai and miniatures, paint with methylated spirits. Cut out any badly-infested, and dying, shoots.
Weevils (clay coloured and vine)	The creamy white or pale brown immature grubs feed on the roots of virtually any plant. Plants wilt and die. Adult weevils feed on the foliage during the night. Keep a special watch on azaleas, rhododendrons and camellias.	Where leaf damage is evident, spray with insecticide and soil drench around the plants. Knock plants out of their containers and remove the grubs by hand. Drench with insecticide before re-potting.
Woolly aphid	Trunks, branches and hardened shoots come under attack. The aphid covers itself with a white wool-like substance for protection. The infested wood swells up, and then it often cracks to allow canker and fungal diseases to get a hold. Buds are often blind and surrounded by galls. Wall-trained plants are most at risk.	Spray at regular intervals with insecticide. In small-scale attacks work methylated spirits well into the woolly patches. Cut out badly-affected wood, and use tar oil as for aphid.

CHEMICALS

	Available as	Uses
Fungicides (to control fungal and some bacterial diseases)	Sprays and aerosols	Sprays are popular and effective for problems above ground. Useful too for making into dips when preparing cuttings. Reserve aerosols for small-scale spot treatment of small plants, young trees and Bonsai. They are convenient but expensive.
	Soil drenches	For disinfecting suspect ground prior to planting, and when cleaning up after the removal of diseased plants. Some are suitable for the pre-treatment of seed containers before sowing.
	Dusts and powders	As a preventive when propagating, and liberally prior to and during winter storage. Also for spot treatment of small young plants.
Insecticides (to control aerial soil pests)	Sprays and aerosols	To control insect pests above ground, and to make up dips for cuttings and the like.
	Soil drenches	For disinfecting suspect ground prior to planting. And as a remedial routine measure to keep container plants free of soil pests.
	Dusts and powders	As fungicides. Useful too for dusting alongside hedge bottoms and other likely pest shelters, and as a pre-planting soil treatment.
	Granules	Prior to planting on suspect ground.
Combined fungicides and insecticides	Sprays	Against aerial pests and diseases.
	Soil drenches	Against soil pests and diseases, and for the sterilisation of containers, tools and equipment.
	Sealants and paints	On saw cuts and wounds of ¾in (2cm) and over, to keep out wet, disease and insect pests.

CHEMICALS

	Available as	Uses
Slug killers and baits	Water-on liquids granules and pellets	To keep special plants, and all young plants, constantly protected against slugs and snails. (These are evident by slimy trails, chewed tender shoots, and holed leaves. Seedlings are devoured wholesale. They feed at night.)
Deterrents	Sprays, dusts, granules, pellets, capsules and buds	For a degree of short-term protection against birds and animals, both wild and domestic.

NUTRITIONAL DISORDERS

	Symptoms	Treatment
Magnesium deficiency	Yellowing between veins	3oz of Magnesium Sulphate per I gal (60gm in 4½ litres), used as a foliar spray.
Manganese deficiency	Yellowing between veins	Use balanced fertiliser plus trace elements.
Nitrogen deficiency	Small pale leaves and poor growth	Use high nitrogen balanced liquid feed in the growing season, or 3oz per sq yd (105g per sq m) of 7:7:7 balanced fertiliser as a dry top dressing.
Potash deficiency	Reddening or purpling of leaf margins	Use high potash liquid feed in the growing season, or 4oz per sq yd (140g per sq m) 7:7:7 balanced fertiliser as a dry top dressing.
Nitrogen excess	Excessive leaf growth	Withhold feed with woody plants for at least a season, and until growth slows down with herbaceous perennials.

Plant Reference Section

I   NAME GUIDE

BOTANICAL	POPULAR
Abutilon	Flowering Maple
Acaena	Burr
Acer	Maple
Alternanthera (Telanthera)	Joy-Weed
Antennaria	Cat's-Ear
Ardisia	Coral Berry
Aubrieta	Aubrieta
Beloperone	Shrimp Plant
Berberis	Barberry
Betula	Birch
Bougainvillea	Bougainvillea
Buddleia	Butterfly Bush
Buxus	Box
Calluna	Heather
Camellia	Camellia
Carex	Sedge
Carissa	Natal Plum
Ceanothus	Californian Lilac
Chaenomeles	Flowering Quince
Chamaecyparis	False Cypress
Chrysanthemum	Marguerite
Clematis	Virgin's Bower
Coleus	Flame Nettle
Corylus	Hazel
Cotoneaster	Cotoneaster
Crataegus	Thorn
Crinodendron	Lantern Tree
Cupressus	Cypress
Cytisus	Broom
Echeveria	Echeveria
Elaeagnus	Oleaster
Erica	Heath, Heather
Escallonia	Escallonia
Euonymus	Spindle
Euphorbia	Scarlet Plume

BOTANICAL	POPULAR
Fagus	Beech
Festuca	Fescus
Ficus	Fig
Forsythia	Golden Bell Bush
Fuchsia	Ladies' Ear-Drops
Garrya	Garrya
Glechoma	Ground Ivy
Griselinia	New Zealand Broad-Leaf
Hedera	Ivy
Heliotropium	Heliotrope
Herniaria	Rupture-Wort
Hibiscus	Tree Mallow
Humulus	Hop
Ilex	Holly
Impatiens	Busy Lizzie
Ipomoea	Morning Glory
Jasminum	Jasmine
Juniperus	Juniper
Laburnum	Golden Chains
Lantana	Lantana
Laurus	Bay
Lavandula	Lavender
Ligustrum	Privet
Lobelia	Lobelia
Lonicera	Evergreen Honeysuckle
Lysimachia	Creeping Jenny
Malus	Apple, Crab Apple
Manettia	Firecracker
Minuartia	Alsine, Sandwort
Myrtus	Myrtle
Olearia	Daisy Bush
Osmanthus	Osmanthus
Parthenocissus	Virginia Creeper
Passiflora	Passion Flower
Pelargonium	Geranium
Perilla	Perilla
Piptanthus	Evergreen Laburnum
Pittosporum	Pittosporum

BOTANICAL	POPULAR
Plumbago	Leadwort
Potentilla	Potentilla
Prunus	Apricot, Cherry, Plum, Peach and Laurel
Punica	Pomegranate
Pyracantha	Firethorn
Pyrus	Pear
Rhododendron	Azalea, Rhododendron
Rhoicissus	Grape Ivy
Rhus	Sumach
Ribes	Flowering Currant
Rosa	Rose
Rosmarinus	Rosemary
Sagina	Pearlwort
Salix	Willow
Salvia	Sage
Sambucus	Golden Cut-Leaf Elder
Santolina	Lavender Cotton
Saxifraga	Saxifrage
Scleranthus	Scleranthus
Sedum	Stonecrop
Sempervivum	House-Leek
Senecio	Senecio
Soleirolia	Helxine, Mind-Your-Own-Business
Sorbus	Mountain Ash
Spiraea	Spiraea, Bridal Wreath
Streptosolen	Streptosolen
Syringa	Lilac
Taxus	Yew
Thuja	Arbor-Vitae
Tilia	Lime
Viburnum	Laurustinus
Vitis	Vine
Wisteria	Wisteria

II PLANTS FOR SPECIAL PURPOSES

Topiary Specimens

BROAD-LEAVED
Berberis x *stenophylla*
Buxus
Cotoneaster

Elaeagnus
Euonymus japonicus
Fagus
Forsythia
Ilex
Laurus
Ligustrum
Olearia
Prunus (plum)
Pyracantha
Santolina

CONIFERS
Chamaecyparis
Juniperus
Taxus

Topiary Miniatures

Buxus
Chamaecyparis
Cotoneaster
Ilex crenata
Juniperus
Ligustrum
Santolina

Topiary Hedging (H) and Edging (E)

BROAD-LEAVED
Berberis (H)
Buxus (H)(E)
Calluna (E)
Cassinia (H)
Cotoneaster (H)
Crataegus (H)
Erica (E)
Escallonia (H)
Euonymus (H)
Fagus (H)
Forsythia (H)
Griselinia (H)
Ilex (H)
Laurus (H)
Lavandula (H)(E)
Ligustrum (H)
Lonicera (H)(E)
Malus (H)

Myrtus (H)
Olearia (H)
Osmarea (H)
Potentilla (H)
Prunus (H)
Pyracantha (H)
Rhododendron (H)
Ribes (H)
Rosmarinus (H)(E)
Salvia (E)
Santolina (H)(E)
Spiraea (H)

CONIFERS
Chamaecyparis (H)
Cupressus (H)
Juniperus (H)
Taxus (H)
Thuja (H)

HARDY PERENNIALS
Carex (E)
Festuca (E)

Topiary Arches (A) and Pleaching (P)

Buxus (A)
Cotoneaster (A)
Fagus (A)(P)
Ilex (A)
Ligustrum (A)
Prunus (A)(P)
Pyracantha (A)
Taxus (A)
Tilia (P)

Wall Topiary

Berberis
Buxus
Cassinia
Cotoneaster
Escallonia
Euonymus
Garrya
Hedera
Myrtus

Parthenocissus
Pyracantha

Carpet Bed Sculptures

HARDY PERENNIALS
Acaena
Antennaria
Aubrieta
Festuca
Lysimachia
Minuartia
Saxifraga
Sedum
Sempervivum

HALF-HARDY PLANTS
Alternanthera
Echeveria
Glechoma
Herniaria
Impatiens
Lobelia
Sagina
Scleranthus
Sedum
Soleirolia

Pinch and Prune Sculptures

SOFTWOOD STANDARDS – TRADITIONAL
Abutilon
Chrysanthemum
Coleus
Fuchsia
Heliotropium
Lantana
Pelargonium
Perilla
Streptosolen

SOFTWOOD STANDARDS – MULTI-STEMMED
Ficus
Hedera
Jasminum
Plumbago
Rhoicissus
Senecio

SOFTWOOD PYRAMIDS – TRADITIONAL
Abutilon
Coleus
Fuchsia
Streptosolen

SOFTWOOD PYRAMIDS – MULTI-STEMMED
Ficus
Hedera
Ipomoea
Lathyrus
Manettia
Passiflora
Rhoicissus
Senecio

SOFTWOOD CORDONS
Ipomoea
Lathyrus
Manettia
Passiflora
Plumbago
Senecio

HARDWOOD STANDARDS – TRADITIONAL
Acer
Betula
Buddleia
Buxus
Cotoneaster
Crataegus
Cytisus
Elaeagnus
Euonymus
Fagus
Hibiscus
Ilex
Laburnum
Laurus
Ligustrum
Malus
Myrtus
Prunus
Pyrus
Rhododendron
Salix
Sorbus
Syringa

Taxus
Tilia
Wisteria

HARDWOOD STANDARDS – MINIATURES
Buxus
Cotoneaster
Ilex
Lonicera
Rosmarinus

HARDWOOD PYRAMIDS – TRADITIONAL
Buxus
Cassinia
Cotoneaster
Euonymus
Fagus
Griselinia
Ilex
Laurus
Ligustrum
Lonicera
Malus
Myrtus
Olearia
Prunus
Pyracantha
Sorbus

HARDWOOD PYRAMIDS – MINIATURES
Buxus
Cassinia
Cotoneaster
Ilex
Lonicera

HARDWOOD SPINDLE BUSH
Chaenomeles
Cotoneaster
Crataegus
Ilex
Malus
Pyracantha
Sorbus
Syringa

HARDWOOD FESTOONS
Chaenomeles
Malus
Prunus (cherry and plum)

HARDWOOD BONSAI AND MINIATURES
Acer
Berberis
Betula
Buxus
Cassinia
Chaenomeles
Cotoneaster
Euonymus
Ligustrum
Piptanthus
Prunus
Pyracantha
Pyrus
Rhododendron
Sorbus

**HARDWOOD WALL-TRAINED FORMS –
CORDONS**
Cotoneaster
Malus
Pyrus

**HARDWOOD WALL-TRAINED FORMS –
ESPALIER**
Cotoneaster
Forsythia
Laburnum
Laurus
Malus
Prunus (laurel)

HARDWOOD WALL-TRAINED FORMS – FAN
Cotoneaster
Cytisus
Malus
Prunus (cherry, peach and plum)
Pyrus
Rosa

**HARDWOOD TRACERY AND TREILLAGE –
HARDY TREES, SHRUBS AND CLIMBERS**
Berberis
Chaenomeles
Clematis
Cotoneaster
Cytisus
Escallonia
Euonymus
Garrya
Hedera
Humulus
Jasminum
Laburnum
Parthenocissus
Piptanthus
Pyracantha
Rosa
Vitis
Wisteria

**HARDWOOD TRACERY AND TREILLAGE –
HALF-HARDY PLANTS**
Abutilon
Ficus
Fuchsia
Ipomoea
Jasminum
Passiflora
Pelargonium
Plumbago
Rhoicissus
Senecio

III   HARDY TREES, SHRUBS AND CLIMBERS

ACER (MAPLE)

Recommended *Acer palmatum* and varieties
Use Good as a free-standing pinch and prune standard. A good Bonsai subject. Grow in containers or plant direct.
Description A small deciduous tree, noted for the brilliance of its red, orange and yellow

The gardens at Oldway Mansions, Paignton, Devon, looking over the elaborate and colourful parterre towards eight huge clipped topiary cones.

A delightful parterre incorporating heart-shaped beds at Abbotswood, Stow-on-the-Wold, Gloucestershire. The creator has successfully combined the jewel colours of blue and pink for a stunning display in the spring.

A massive hedge clipped to form a solid archway over a small gate in Sapperton, Gloucestershire.

A clipped hedge forms an effective and striking window frame for a Cotswold-stone house alongside the river at Lower Slaughter.

Trained hedging 'hugging' the porch of a beautiful house at Westwell, Oxfordshire.

Two yew peacocks adorn the hedge between the Fuchsia Garden and
the Bathing Pool Garden at Hidcote Manor, Gloucestershire.

A trained and clipped topiary duck creates a talking point in this garden
at Wickhambrook, Suffolk.

'Old Nessie', a much-loved box hedge in a town garden in Quinton, near Birmingham.

A mature topiary cakestand partly obscured by a fine stone wall in Hinksey, Oxfordshire.

autumn leaf tints. Ht and Sp 10–13ft (3–4m). **Treatment** Does well in a sunny spot, partially shaded from fierce midday sun. Shelter from cold, drying winds – not a tree for exposed gardens. Colours best on acid soil – use containers if your soil is shallow and chalky. Keep young plants well watered and mist over foliage in dry weather. Protect roots from frost – container-grown plants are most at risk. Remove suckers promptly. Pinch and prune to shape, but don't cut in later winter, otherwise you risk bleeding.

Propagation Mainly commercially by budding and grafting.

BERBERIS (BARBERRY)

Recommended *Berberis x stenophylla*

Use As a free-standing topiary specimen and for hedging, wall topiary and tracery. Useful for Bonsai work too. Best direct-planted, Bonsai excepted.

Description Evergreen shrub with golden spring flowers. Ht 8ft (2.4m), Sp 6ft (1.8m).

Treatment Suitable for sun and semi-shade. Avoid east-facing sites to minimise frost injury. Any reasonable soil will do, and this shrub stands chalk. Once established, it will also tolerate dry soil. During the early years keep the base free of weeds to avoid a jungle and the subsequent danger of bare stems. Clip in spring and summer.

Propagation Relatively easy from autumn-sown and self-sown seeds. Semi-ripe wood cuttings taken in August and ripe wood cuttings taken in September should present few problems for those with a frame.

BERBERIS (BARBERRY)

Recommended *Berberis thunbergii* and varieties

Use As a free-standing topiary specimen, and for hedging, wall topiary and tracery. Suitable too for Bonsai. Best direct-planted, Bonsai excepted.

Description Deciduous shrub with yellow spring flowers and red autumn berries. Red and gold autumn leaf tints. Ht 5ft (1.5m), Sp 4ft (1.2m).

Treatment Thrives in sun and semi-shade. Any reasonable soil will do, and stands chalk. Tolerates dry soil once established. A good shrub for exposed gardens. Keep the base weed-free in the early days to encourage branching low down. Clip in spring, summer and autumn.

Propagation Relatively easy from autumn-sown and self-sown seeds. Those with a frame could take semi-ripe cuttings in August and ripe wood cuttings in September.

BETULA (BIRCH)

Recommended *Betula pendula* and varieties

Use As pinch and prune specimen standards. Normally direct-planted but can be grown in containers. Make good Bonsai.

Description Attractive, white-barked deciduous trees with yellow autumn tints. Ht and Sp 10–12ft (3–6m).

Treatment Does well in sun and in partial or light shade. Any reasonable spot will suffice, but do avoid planting in very exposed gardens. Average soil is adequate – stands chalk and survives shallow soil of 12in (30cm) or so. Tolerant of both dryish and very moist soils. Syringe the foliage of newly-planted trees in first summer, and stake young standards early. Pinch and prune to form main framework, thereafter minimal work required once established, except for Bonsai. Avoid pruning in late winter or spring as trees bleed.

Propagation Best budded or grafted by growers. Weeping standards must be top-worked. Common birch can be raised from seed.

BUDDLEIA (BUTTERFLY BUSH)

Recommended *Buddleia alternifolia*
Use As a pinch and prune standard, or wall tracery. Possible, though not usual, as a container plant.
Description A lovely deciduous shrub with scented purple summer flowers on arching branches. Attracts butterflies. Ht 10ft (3m), Sp 8ft (2.5m).
Treatment Needs sun, and shelter is essential in cold gardens. Don't plant in hard winter areas nor in exposed sites. Well-drained, dryish, chalky soil is preferred – avoid heavy, wet soil. Provide permanent staking in all but the most sheltered spots. Needs careful formation training. Subsequently shorten back flowered shoots in early autumn.
Propagation Semi-ripe cuttings taken in July/August will root on an indoor window-sill in the absence of a cold frame.

BUXUS (BOX)

Recommended *Buxus sempervirens* and varieties
Use For topiary. Outstanding as standards and bird, animal or geometrical shapes. Ideal for arches, hedging, edging and wall topiary. Good in containers. Excellent for Bonsai and miniatures.
Description Slow-growing evergreen tree or shrub with aromatic glossy green or variegated foliage. Ht up to 15ft (4.5m), Sp up to 9ft (2.8m).
Treatment Suitable for most areas, for sunny, semi or partially shaded spots. To minimise the risk of scorch in cold areas avoid planting in north- or east-facing beds open to freezing, drying winds. Any reasonable soil will do – does well on chalk. Tolerant of dryish soils once established. Clip during late spring and summer. Start training early to encourage a bushy base.

Propagation Semi-ripe cuttings taken in July/August will root under a cold frame, cloche or on an indoor window-sill.

CALLUNA (HEATHER)

Recommended *Calluna vulgaris* and varieties
Use As topiary, mainly as an edging but has possibilities as low hedging. Plant direct – fickle in containers.
Description Attractive, dwarf evergreen shrubs with pink, red, white or purple summer/autumn flowers – some have variegated foliage. Ht and Sp 12–24in (30–60cm).
Treatment Plant in a sunny, open aspect. Very hardy and useful in exposed situations. Acid, peaty soil is necessary. Needs a moist root run until established, thereafter stands dryish summer conditions. Give generous peat mulches in early years. Essential to plant in weed-free soil. Clip after flowering in autumn or spring – make it spring where winter foliage is a feature.
Propagation Take 1½in (4cm) semi-ripe tip cuttings in summer – root in good light under cover. Alternatively, layer in spring.

CAMELLIA (CAMELLIA)

Recommended *Camellia japonica* and varieties
Use For pinch and prune standards, pyramids and wall treillage. Does well both planted direct and in containers.
Description Popular, slow-growing evergreen shrubs with leathery, glossy leaves. The exotic, waxy flowers come in singles, semi-doubles and doubles, in shades of white, pink and red – self, bi-coloured and multi-coloured. They appear in late winter or spring. Ht and Sp up to 5ft (1.5m).
Treatment A suitable shrub for a dappled or partially-shaded sheltered spot. Grow outdoors in mild areas; treat as a half-hardy

plant in cold areas or exposed gardens. Thrives in acid, peaty, reasonably fertile soil which is not over-rich – resents lime. Keep roots moist, giving priority for mulching. Young plants should be sprayed over daily with rain water during hot, dry weather. Prune after flowering in spring. After initial training and shaping keep pruning to a miniumum, otherwise you risk losing a year's flowers.

Overwintering Outdoors *in situ* in mild areas. Otherwise move into a cool greenhouse or conservatory and maintain a temperature of 41–45°F (5–7°C).

Propagation Take semi-ripe wood cuttings in summer and root in warmth at 60°F (16°C).

CASSINIA (GOLDEN BUSH)

Recommended *Cassinia fulvida*

Use As wall topiary and hedging, and as pinch and prune pyramids. Can be grown in containers as short pinch and prune standards, and as miniature standards and pyramids. Useful for Bonsai.

Description Evergreen shrub with fine-leaved golden foliage and white flowers in July. Ht and Sp 4ft (1.2m).

Treatment Needs a sunny, sheltered spot – not for harsh, cold climates. Light to medium free-draining soil is preferred, and will survive on good topsoil overlying chalk. Use soil-based potting compost in containers. Clip or prune after flowering.

Propagation Take semi-ripe cuttings in late summer and root under a frame.

CEANOTHUS (CALIFORNIAN LILAC)

Recommended *Ceanothus dentatus*

Use For pinch and prune standards and wall treillage. Best direct-planted, difficult to manage in containers.

Description A moderately hardy, medium to slow-growing evergreen shrub with tiny leaves. It is noted for its attractive blue flowers during May and June. Ht and Sp up to 10ft (3m).

Treatment Grow in full sun, in a south- or west-facing sheltered position. An ideal shrub for a mild climate. Grow with the protection of a warm wall in cold areas or exposed gardens. Any well-drained light to medium soil of average fertility will suffice – tolerant of chalk. Permanent supports are needed. When training young plants, pinch and prune during spring and summer. Mature plants are pruned after flowering.

Propagation Take semi-ripe wood cuttings in summer and root in warmth at 60°F (16°C).

Note In cold districts, both roots and tops should be protected from frost.

CHAENOMELES (FLOWERING QUINCE)

Recommended *Chaenomeles speciosa* and varieties
Chaenomeles x superba and varieties

Use As a pinch and prune free-standing spindle bush, festoon, wall tracery or as Bonsai. Best planted *in situ*.

Description Deciduous shrub with pink, red and white flowers in late winter/spring. Ht 4–8ft (1.2–2.5m), Sp 3½–7ft (1–2m).

Treatment Suitable for sun or semi-shade and for most areas, but is best grown on a warm wall in hard winter sites. Average soil is adequate – stands chalk and heavy soils. Provided they are drained, very moist soils are tolerated. Avoid planting in or feeding plants in over-rich soils. Routine summer prune. Root prune over-vigorous plants.

Propagation Pin down layers in autumn or spring.

CLEMATIS (VIRGIN'S BOWER)

Recommended Large-flowered clematis
varieties
Clematis montana varieties

Use As pinch and prune tracery. Best planted *in situ*.

Description Pretty deciduous climbers with single and bi-coloured flowers in shades of red, pink, white, purple and mauve freely produced in spring and summer. Ht 8–20ft (2.5–6m), Sp 4–15ft (1.2–4.5m).

Treatment Suitable for sunny and partially shaded aspects. Don't plant in areas with cold winter climates – critical for evergreens – and in milder areas don't plant evergreens on east-facing walls. Chalky or well-limed soil is preferred – it should be deep, cool and moist, but well drained. Mulch generously and keep roots cool. After clematis wilt allow a 2–3 year interval before replanting. With large-flowered varieties, cut flowered shoots back to the main framework in late winter and tie in replacement shoots. In the case of *C. montana* cut out flowered shoots in June, again training in new shoots.

Propagation Take semi-ripe wood inter-node cuttings in summer and root indoors or under a frame.

CORYLUS (HAZEL)

Recommended *Corylus avellana* varieties
Corylus maxima 'Purpurea'

Use As pinch and prune hedging. A very limited scope in containers.

Description Deciduous shrubs, noted for their yellow spring catkins and large green or purple leaves turning yellow in autumn. Ht 10ft (3m), Sp 7ft (2m).

Treatment Suitable for sun or semi-shade, but good growth and size is only likely in mild climates. Any reasonable free-draining soil will do – stands chalk. Avoid over-rich soil if catkin production and autumn leaf colour are to be at their best. Although hazel enjoys a moist root run, avoid planting in soils which tend to waterlog. Routine prune in summer and autumn.

Propagation Pin down layers in spring.

COTONEASTER (COTONEASTER)

Recommended *Cotoneaster* 'Hybridus
Pendulus'
Cotoneaster horizontalis
Cotoneaster lacteus
*Cotoneaster salicifolius
floccosus*

Uses As topiary, use *C. lacteus* for free-standing sculptures, hedging, arches and wall topiaries, and *C. horizontalis* for minatures. Pinch and prune – use *C. 'Hybridus Pendulus'* for weeping standards; *C. lacteus* for traditional standards and pyramids, spindle bush, and wall forms; *C. horizontalis* for miniature standards and pyramids, Bonsai and miniatures; and *C. salicifolius floccosus* for wall forms and tracery. Suitable for direct planting and container work. Ht and Sp up to 10ft (3m), *C. horizontalis* excepted (ht 5ft (1.5m)).

Description Versatile shrubs with white summer flowers and red autumn berries into winter. *C. horizontalis* is deciduous, others are evergreen or semi-evergreen.

Treatment Hardy in most areas in sun and semi-shade. Any average soil will do, but moist, well-drained soil preferred. Once established will tolerate dry soil in summer – good on chalk. Cut out woolly aphid on sight. Clip topiary in spring and summer. Pinch and prune in summer and early autumn.

Propagation *C. 'Hybridus Pendulus'* is top-worked or grafted commercially for weeping trees. Semi-ripe wood cuttings of the remainder, taken in summer, will root well under cover.

CRATAEGUS (THORN)

Recommended *Crataegus* and varieties
Crataegus prunifolia
Use *C. oxyacantha* and varieties as topiary hedging. All are suitable for pinch and prune traditional standards and spindle bushes. Plant direct or grow in containers.
Description Deciduous trees and shrubs with scented May/June white, pink or red flowers, and red autumn/winter berries. Ht and Sp up to 18ft (5m).
Treatment Best in sun – worthwhile in semi-shade. Hardy in most areas, but tends to become misshapen in exposed, windswept gardens. A fertile, not-too-rich soil is preferred. Once established will tolerate dryish to very moist soils, if well drained. Support traditional standards for at least 5 years after planting. Summer prune after flowering, but not before. Thin out crowns of standards every 3 years. Clip topiary in summer/early autumn. Summer prune spindle bush. Summer and winter prune traditional standards.
Propagation Varieties of *C. oxyacantha* are best budded or grafted by the grower. *C. oxyacantha* and *C. prunifolia* species can be raised from seed down in autumn in a cold frame.

CRINODENDRON (LANTERN TREE)

Recommended *Crinodendron hookerianum*
Use For pinch and prune standards and wall treillage. Best planted direct but will adapt to containers if there is no other alternative.
Description A choice, spectacular, slow-growing evergreen shrub or small tree. It has deep rich-green leaves and masses of pendant bright crimson flowers during May and June. Ht up to 8ft (2.5m), Sp up to 5ft (1.5m).
Treatment Lantern tree is only really suitable for mild climates. Don't plant in cold areas or exposed gardens. Choose a dapple-shaded, preferably west-facing, sheltered spot, out of the wind and strong sun. Does best on acid, peaty or leafy soil of average fertility – nothing too rich. Don't plant on chalky soil. A moist root run is essential, so give priority for mulching, and use rain water for irrigation in hard water areas. Overwinter outdoors – the roots of young plants will need extra protection. Move container-grown shrubs into a cool greenhouse or conservatory where a temperature of around 45°F (7°C) can be maintained. Pinch and prune during spring and summer.
Propagation Take semi-ripe wood cuttings in summer and root in warmth at 60°F (16°C).
Note This shrub is difficult to obtain, but it is well worth the trouble of tracking it down.

CYTISUS (BROOM)

Recommended *Cytisus battandieri*
Cytisus praecox and
varieties
Cytisus scoparius and
varieties
Uses Varieties of *C. scoparius* and *C. praecox* for topiary standards. *C. battandieri* for pinch and prune free-standing standards and wall-trained fan and tracery. All are best grown *in situ*.
Description Quick-growing deciduous shrubs, or a small tree in the case of *C. battandieri*. All are short-lived and flower May–June. *C. battandieri* has scented golden flowers; *C. scoparius* has varieties in red, cream, gold and bronze; and *C. praecox* varieties come in gold or white. Ht and Sp 5ft (1.5m) – *C. battandieri* is the exception, Ht 10ft (3m) Sp 7ft (2m).
Treatment Sunny position is essential. Not for cold or exposed gardens. Lightish, well-drained soil is preferred – once established, brooms enjoy dryish root conditions in

summer, and all resent root disturbance. Summer prune *C. battandieri* and clip over the others during summer as well.

Propagation Raise species *C. battandieri*, *C. praecox* and *C. scoparius* from seed sown under cover in summer. Sow singly in small pots. Take heel cuttings of named varieties in July.

ELAEAGNUS (OLEASTER)

Recommended Varieties of *Elaeagnus pungens*

Use As topiary standards and hedging, and as pinch and prune standards. Good in containers.

Description Outstanding moderate- to slow-growing evergreen foliage shrub with bold silver or gold leathery variegated leaves. Ht and Sp 5–10ft (1.5–3m).

Treatment Does best in sun, but partial shade is tolerated. Mild climate areas preferred. Needs shelter and protection from freezing east winds in cold exposed gardens. Avoid planting on heavy wet land. Light to medium well-drained soil is ideal – stands chalk if topsoil is fertile. Regular watering and syringing over in hot, dry weather for 1–2 years after planting repays well. Cut out reverted green shoots on sight, any time except during hard frosts. Aim to clip or prune during summer.

Propagation Take semi-ripe wood cuttings in summer and root under a frame or on an indoor window-sill.

ERICA (HEATH AND HEATHER)

Recommended *E. carnea*, *E. ciliaris* and *E. vagans* are particularly good

Use Excellent for topiary edging. *E. carnea* varieties tolerate container growing, others are best planted direct.

Description First-class medium to slow-growing evergreen shrubs, some with most attractive variegated foilage. *E. carnea* is winter/spring flowering. Others bloom in summer and autumn. All come in shades of pink, red, white, purple and mauve. Ht 6–24in (15–60cm), Sp 12–24in (30–60cm).

Treatment A sunny, open, unshaded aspect is ideal. Hardy and useful for cold gardens. An acid, peaty soil is needed – fertile but not over-rich. *E. carnea* will stand some chalk. A moist, cool root run is preferred, mulch generously with peat in the early years. Use rain water for irrigation in hard water areas. If wilt attacks, remove dead plant *plus* soil and drench hole with fungicide as makers direct, before gapping up. Clip over after flowering. Where winter foliage colour is paramount, defer clipping of late summer/autumn flowering varieties until spring.

Propagation As *Calluna*.

ESCALLONIA (ESCALLONIA)

Recommended *Escallonia* 'C F Ball'
Escallonia 'Iveyi'

Use As topiary hedging and wall cover, and as pinch and prune tracery. Not recommended for containers unless there is no other alternative.

Description Useful medium to quick-growing semi-evergreen/evergreen shrub with pink, red or white summer flowers. Ht 5–10ft (1.5–3m), Sp 5–7ft (1.5–2m).

Treatment Prefers sun, but does reasonably well in partial shade. Escallonia is best reserved for mild climate areas. Any average light to medium well-drained soil will do. A moist root run is needed, especially for newly-planted shrubs in their first year, so mulch generously. If frosted in a hard winter, cut back hard to live wood and retrain. Routine clip or prune after flowering in summer.

Propagation Take semi-ripe wood cuttings in July/August and root under cover.

EUONYMUS (SPINDLE)

Recommended Varieties of *Euonymus fortunei*
Varieties of *Euonymus japonicus*

Use Varieties of *E. japonicus* for topiary standards and hedging, and for pinch and prune standards and pyramids. Varieties of *E. fortunei* are good for wall topiary, wall tracery and Bonsai. Suitable for both containers and direct planting.

Description Attractive medium to slow-growing evergreen shrubs with plain green foliage or silver or gold variegated leaves. A few varieties of *E. fortunei* are climbers. *E. japonicus* Ht 7ft (2m), Sp 5ft (1.5m); *E. fortunei* Ht 1–6ft (30–180cm), Sp 2–8ft (60cm–2.5m).

Treatment Does well in sun, dappled or semi-shade and in mild, moist climates. Also bears up to coastal winds in moderation. Keep watered and spray over foliage until established. Once established adapts to most soils from light sandy to clay, if drained, and stands chalk. Start to train up and support climbing varieties as soon as they are big enough to handle. Routine clip or prune in summer.

Propagation Take semi-ripe wood cuttings in July/August. Root under cover, in a frame, plastic-covered box or on an indoor sill.

FAGUS (BEECH)

Recommended Varieties of *Fagus sylvatica*

Use For topiary sculptures, arches, pleaching and hedging, and for pinching and prune standards, weeping standards and pyramids. Best planted direct.

Description Slow-growing deciduous foliage trees with green, pale yellow, copper or purple foliage. Weeping forms available. Ht up to 35ft (7.5m) plus; Sp up to 20ft (6m) plus.

Treatment Coloured varieties colour best in sun. Dappled sun is fine for green-leaved varieties. Hardy in most areas. Any average soil will suffice but deep moist soil is best. Good on chalk. Water and spray over newly-planted trees for the first year or two during hot weather. With topiary features, regular close clipping is needed to provide a dense texture. Routine clip and prune in summer – prune in autumn.

Propagation Sow common beach, *F. sylvatica* in autumn under frames. Coloured and weeping forms are grafted commercially in spring.

FORSYTHIA (GOLDEN BELL BUSH)

Recommended *Forsythia x intermedia* and varieties
Forsythia suspensa

Use *F. x intermedia* and varieties for topiary standards, pyramids, other sculptures and hedging. *F. suspensa* makes a good pinch and prune sculpture. All are best planted direct.

Description Deciduous, quick-growing, spring-flowering shrubs in shades of yellow. Ht and Sp 6–10ft (1.8–3m).

Treatment Best in sun, but stands dappled shade. Very hardy, bears up well to wind. Any average soil will do – adapts well to heavy as well as light soils. Avoid over-rich soils – they will encourage fewer flowers. To rejuvenate old shrubs, cut hard back in autumn and then be prepared to wait up to three years to come back into full flower. Start clipping or pruning in late spring after flowering.

Propagation Take semi-ripe wood cuttings in July/August and root under cover. Take ripe wood cuttings in October/November.

GARRYA (GARRYA)

Recommended *Garrya elliptica*

Use For wall topiaries as well as pinch and prune tracery. Best planted direct.

Description A curious medium to fast-growing evergreen shrub, with dark green glossy leaves and long late winter catkins. For the longest catkins choose male or selected varieties. Ht 10–12ft (3–3.5m), Sp 8–10ft (2.5–3m).

Treatment Does well in dappled or semi-shade. Although hardy, benefits from a sheltered spot in cold areas. Any average, reasonably fertile soil is fine – adapts to chalk. Mulch to encourage steady growth. Support plants in early years at least. Start clipping and pruning in summer.

Propagation Take semi-ripe wood cuttings in August and root under a frame or on an indoor sill.

GRISELINIA (NEW ZEALAND BROAD-LEAF)

Recommended *Griselinia littoralis*
Griselinia littoralis 'Variegata'

Use As topiary hedging and pinch and prune standards and pyramids. Plant direct or in containers.

Description Attractive, slow-growing, ever-green foliage shrubs with largish, glossy green or white variegated leaves. Ht 6–10ft (1.8–3m), Sp 4–6ft (1.2–8m).

Treatment Grows well in sun, dappled shade or semi-shade. Slightly frost-tender – not for exposed gardens. Average light to medium soil preferred, and chalk is tolerated. Variegated variety is slower-growing, smaller and more tender than the green-leaved form, and so best reserved for mild areas. All enjoy a moist root run, so mulch generously. Spray over foliage in hot dry weather in the first summer after planting. With the variegated form cut out reverted green shoots on sight. Start clipping and pruning in late spring.

Propagation Take semi-ripe wood cuttings in July/August and root in a frame or on an indoor window-sill.

HEDERA (IVY)

Recommended *Hedera helix* and varieties
Use For wall topiaries, pinch and prune multi-stemmed standards and wall tracery. Plant direct or in containers.

Description Highly popular medium to slow-growing evergreen climbers with leathery, glossy leaves. Plain green and variegated forms with white or gold markings are available. Ht and Sp up to 15ft (4.5m).

Treatment Not fussy, does well in sun, dappled or semi-shade. Although very hardy, ivies are at their best in mild, moist conditions. Any reasonably fertile soil will do – stands chalk. A moist root run is needed until established, when able to grow in varying conditions from dryish to very moist – so mulch generously in early stages, and spray over in hot dry weather. Permanent supports are needed – they should be secured 1in (3cm) out from the wall. Be on guard against scale insects, especially with indoor sculptures. Start clipping and pruning in late spring and continue through summer as necessary.

Propagation Semi-ripe wood cuttings taken in summer root readily under cover.

HIBISCUS (TREE MALLOW)

Recommended Varieties of *Hibiscus syriacus*
Use For pinch and prune standards. Suitable for direct planting and container growing.

Description Outstanding slow-growing deciduous shrubs with large bi-coloured autumn flowers in shades of blue, pink and carmine, all with red blotches. Ht and Sp 5–8ft (1.5–2.5m).

Treatment Needs a warm, sunny site – best where summers are hot. Not for areas with harsh winter climates. Grow in average to good, reasonably fertile soil. Chalky soil tolerated. Water and mulch during the first year after planting to ensure adequate moisture. Provide permanent support.

Shorten back side-shoots in summer, leaving flower buds intact. Autumn prune after flowering is over.

Propagation Semi-ripe wood heel cuttings, taken in July/August will root in warmth at 60°F (16°C).

HUMULUS (HOP)

Recommended *Humulus lupulus* 'Aureus'

Use For pinch and prune multi-stemmed pyramids, for training over free-standing tripods, and for treillage. Best direct-planted, but worth trying in containers where there is no other option.

Description A quick-growing deciduous climber grown for its pale golden leaves. Ht 10–13ft (3–4m), Sp 3–7ft (1–2m).

Treatment Needs sun and shelter from strong winds. Most suitable for mild areas. Any soil of average fertility will suffice, but don't plant on shallow soil liable to acute dryness. Protect roots from severe frosts during winter. Ensure that supports are adequate and that shoots are tied in regularly. Pinch back side-shoots during summer and take out the growing points once the desired height has been reached. In late autumn, cut down the tops, taking them right back to within about 4in (20cm) of soil level.

Propagation Lift and divide in spring.

ILEX (HOLLY)

Recommended *Ilex aquifolium* and varieties
Ilex crenata and varieties

Uses *I. aquifolium* and varieties for topiary standards, pyramids, sculptures, arches, pleaching and hedging. Use both *I. aquifolium* and *I. crenata* (and varieties) for pinch and prune standards, weeping standards and pyramids. Use *I. crenata* and varieties for topiary, pinch and prune miniature standards and pyramids, and Bonsai. Best planted direct but will adapt to containers.

Description Ever-popular, slow-growing, evergreen trees and shrubs. Leaves leathery green or gold, plus white and gold variegated varieties. Red autumn and winter berries. Check berrying – male and female plants may be needed. Ht 3–10ft (1–3m), Sp 3–7ft (1–2m).

Treatment Give variegated and coloured varieties a sunny spot – green-leaved forms will tolerate dappled and semi-shade. Hardy and suited to most areas. Average to fertile soil is best; heavy soil suitable. Avoid extremes of moisture or dryness. Water regularly in dry spells during the first year, and ensure adequate feed and moisture throughout the formation training period. Clip and prune in spring and summer.

Propagation Raise common holly from seed sown in autumn under cover. Take semi-ripe heel cuttings in July of named varieties (weeping forms excepted) and root under a frame. Weeping varieties are budded or grafted commercially.

JASMINUM (JASMINE)

Recommended *Jasminum nudiflorum*
Jasminum officinale

Use *J. officinale* for pinch and prune multi-stem standards and pyramids. Use both *J. nudiflorum* and *J. officinale* for tracery. Best direct-planted but can be grown in containers.

Description Attractive quick-growing deciduous climbers. *J. nudiflorum* is winter/spring flowering in gold. *J. officinale* has sweet-scented white summer flowers. Ht 10–20ft (3–6m), Sp up to 10ft (3m).

Treatment Best in sun and warmth, not for cold exposed sites. Average, reasonably fertile well-drained soil is needed. Grows well over chalk. Keep well watered in first year after planting. Provide permanent supports and tie in, and summer prune to shape.

Propagation Take semi-ripe wood cuttings in August and root under a cold frame.

LABURNUM (GOLDEN CHAINS)

Recommended *Laburnum anagyroides* and varieties

Laburnum x watereri 'Vossii'

Use For pinch and prune standards, wall-trained espaliers, wall tracery, and treillage over covered walks. Plant direct or in containers.

Description Popular moderate to quick-growing deciduous trees, noted for their golden-yellow pendulous racemes in late spring/early summer. Ht up to 18ft (5m), Sp up to 12ft (3.5m).

Treatment Best in sun, but adapts well to dappled shade. Hardy in most areas and stands up well to wind and hard winters. Any reasonable soil will do. Good on chalk, given a minimum 12in (30cm) of good topsoil. Tolerant of heavy soil provided it is not waterlogged. Needs regular watering in first summer after planting and thereafter during formation training. Provide permanent supports for wall tracery and treillage. Pick off poisonous seed pods if children around. Summer prune wall-trained tracery and treillage. Autumn prune standards.

Propagation Raise *L. anagyroides* species from seed sown in autumn under a frame. Named varieties are best grafted commercially.

LAURUS (BAY)

Recommended *Laurus nobilis* and variety 'Aurea'

Use For topiary sculptures including standards, pyramids and hedging, and for pinch and prune standards, pyramids and wall-trained espaliers. Plant direct or grow in containers.

Description One of the best known topiary trees, renowned for their aromatic green foliage and slow growth rate. Ht and Sp 10–20ft (3–6m).

Treatment Best in sun but survives dappled shade. Needs a mild, warm, sheltered site; not for cold winter areas. Average to rich fertile soil is best and chalk no problem. Keep well watered and spray over when newly planted. Once established will tolerate dryish soils in summer. Look out for scale insects. Start clipping or pruning in summer and continue until early autumn.

Propagation Take semi-ripe wood heel cuttings in August and root under cover.

LAVANDULA (LAVENDER)

Recommended 'Hidcote' and 'Munstead' varieties of *Lavandula officinalis*

Use For low topiary hedging and edging especially around knot gardens. Best planted *in situ* but worthwhile in containers.

Description Well-loved evergreen, grey-leaved aromatic shrubs with lavender-blue or purple scented summer flowers. Ht 1–2½ft (30–75cm), Sp 2–2½ft (60–75cm).

Treatment Best in full sun and warm, sheltered gardens. Passable in cool climates but not for extremely cold winter areas. Any average, not over-rich, light to medium soil is fine. Good on chalk. Keep reasonably moist until established. Avoid over-feeding and over-watering. Clip over after flowering and remove flowered heads.

Propagation Take semi-ripe wood cuttings in summer and root under frames or cloches.

LIGUSTRUM (PRIVET)

Recommended *Ligustrum ovalifolium* and variety 'Aureum'
Use For topiary sculptures, standards, pyramids, animals, arches and hedging, plus wall topiaries. Also for pinch and prune standards, pyramids, Bonsai and miniatures. Good in containers as well as direct-planted.
Description Quick-growing semi-evergreen/ evergreen shrubs widely grown for their foliage. *L. ovalifolium* has green foliage; 'Aureum' golden variegated. Ht 6–8ft (1.8–2.5m), Sp 4–5ft (1.2–1.5m).
Treatment Best in light shade, but 'Aureum' especially does well in sun. Hardy and suitable for most areas. Hungry shrub really needs average to rich fertile soil. Good on chalk and tolerant of heavy soils within reason. Versatile once established. Frequent regular clipping or pruning is essential from summer to autumn. Cut out reverted green shoots on 'Aurea' on sight.
Propagation Semi-ripe wood cuttings taken in July/August root well under cover. Take hardwood cuttings in autumn.

LONICERA (EVERGREEN HONEYSUCKLE)

Recommended *Lonicera nitida* and variety 'Baggesons Gold'
Use For topiary hedging, edging and miniature sculptures, plus wall topiaries, and for pinch and prune standard and miniature sculptures. Best planted *in situ* but suitable for containers.
Description Useful evergreen shrubs grown for their foliage texture and colour. *L. nitida* has tiny glossy green leathery leaves; 'Baggesons Gold' is golden variegated. Ht 3½ft–7ft (1–2m), Sp 3–4ft (90–120cm).
Treatment Best in sun (especially 'Baggesons Gold'), but worthwhile in dappled shade if not under the drip of trees. Best reserved for mild

climates, being liable to frost injury in hard winters. Any reasonable soil will do. Water and spray for first year or two, and mulch generously. Regular clipping/pruning, every two to three weeks, is essential if gappiness is to be avoided – start in spring.
Propagation Take semi-ripe wood cuttings in summer and root under frames, or take hardwood cuttings in autumn.

MALUS (APPLE AND CRAB APPLE)

Recommended *Malus* hybrids
Malus sargentii
Use Good as a topiary hedge, but used in the main for pinch and prune standards, pyramids, spindle bushes and festoons, and for wall-trained cordons, espaliers and fans. Best direct-planted but suitable for containers.
Description Deciduous trees of average growth rate, noted for their pink, purple and white spring flowers, and red, crimson or yellow summer and autumn fruits. Ht and Sp 5–20ft (1.5–6m).
Treatment Best in full sun. Hardy in most areas, but if a full fruit set is to be ensured don't plant where exposed or liable to late spring frosts. Any reasonably fertile soil will suffice – avoid over-rich conditions. Chalk presents no problems. Seek advice on the need for pollinator varieties. Prune spindle bushes, festoons and wall forms, and clip topiary hedges in summer. Prune pyramids and standards in late summer or autumn.
Propagation Budded or grafted commercially.

MYRTUS (MYRTLE)

Recommended *Myrtus communis* and varieties ('Tarentina' is particularly good)
Use For topiary hedging, and for pinch and prune standards and pyramids. Best planted direct in warmest areas. Elsewhere grow in

115

containers so that they can be moved indoors in winter.

Description An evergreen, moderate to slow-growing shrub with aromatic dark green glossy leaves and white fragrant summer flowers. Ht 3½–8ft (1–2.5m), Sp 2–10ft (60m–3m).

Treatment A sunny spot and mild climate is essential, free from cold winds. However, mild coastal breezes are tolerated. Light to medium well-drained soil of average to good fertility is required. Protect roots from frost during the first winter. Clip topiary hedges and prune standards and pyramids in summer.

Propagation Take semi-ripe wood heel cuttings in summer and root in warmth at 60–65°F (16–18°C).

OLEARIA (DAISY BUSH)

Recommended *Olearia x haastii*
Olearia macrodonta

Use For topiary standards and pyramids, plus hedging. Plant direct.

Description Moderately quick-growing evergreen shrubs with white daisy-like scented summer flowers. *O. x haastii* has small green leaves with grey reverse. The foliage of *O. macrodonta* is holly-like and sage green; leaf undersides are white. Ht 4–7ft (1.2–2m), Sp 4–6ft (1.2–1.8m).

Treatment Does well in sun or semi-shade. *O. x haastii* is suitable for all but the coldest and most exposed of inland gardens. *O. macrodonta* needs a mild area. Both are very good by the sea. Light to medium well-drained soil of average fertility is preferred, but it will adapt to chalky soil. Shelter all newly-planted shrubs until established. Clip during late spring and summer, and remove old flower heads as they fade to avoid weakening plants.

Propagation Take semi-ripe wood cuttings during summer and root under a cold frame.

OSMAREA (OSMANTHUS)

Recommended *Osmarea x burkwoodii*

Use For topiary sculptures and hedging, and for pinch and prune sculptures. Best planted direct but will adapt to container growing.

Description A moderate to slow-growing evergreen shrub, grown mainly for its glossy foliage. The white spring flowers are a bonus. Ht up to 7ft (2m), Sp up to 4ft (1.2m).

Treatment Although best in partial shade and a west-facing position ideal, osmanthus is worth trying in sunny situations. Suitable for most areas, but don't plant in cold, exposed, windswept sites. Light to medium free-draining soil of average fertility is preferred – chalk is tolerated. Protect the roots of container-grown shrubs during winter. Clip during spring and summer using hand pruners for the first few cuts, otherwise you risk some browning of the largish young leaves.

Propagation Take semi-ripe wood cuttings in later summer and root under a cold frame, or, better still, indoors in warmth.

PARTHENOCISSUS (VIRGINIA CREEPER)

Recommended *Parthenocissus*

Use For wall topiary and pinch and prune wall tracery and treillage. Best planted *in situ* but worthwhile in containers.

Description Quick-growing deciduous foliage climber with attractive pink and silver variegated leaves, turning through brilliant red autumn hues. Ht up to 18ft (5m), Sp up to 10ft (3m).

Treatment Mild climate preferred where it does best on a west to north aspect, but worth trying in most areas. Plant against a south or west wall in cold districts. Any reasonable soil will do. Grow on trellis fixed at least 1in (3cm) out from the wall. Clip or prune in summer or early autumn.

Propagation Semi-ripe wood cuttings taken

in summer should root in warmth at 60–65°F (16–18°F).

PIPTANTHUS (EVERGREEN LABURNUM)

Recommended *Piptanthus laburnifolius*
Use For pinch and prune Bonsai and wall tracery. Plant direct or grow in containers.
Description Uncommon evergreen/semi-evergreen tree or shrub with laburnum-like golden flowers in early summer. Ht to 12ft (3.5m); Sp to 10ft (3m).
Treatment Give priority for a sunny spot. Only suitable for mild climates and fertile, rich soils. Cover roots with straw to give frost protection during the first winter. Prune from spring through to autumn.
Propagation Best bought in but can be raised from seed sown in warmth in spring.

PITTOSPORUM (PITTOSPORUM)

Recommended *Pittosporum tenuifolium*
Use For topiary sculptures, standards and pyramids, and for pinch and prune standards as well as for Bonsai. Good both direct-planted and in containers.
Description An unusual medium to slow-growing evergreen foliage shrub with attractive waved, pale to bright-green leaves on striking black stems. Sweet-scented small, dark purple flowers appear in spring. Ht up to 12ft (3.5m), Sp up to 7ft (2m).
Treatment Only suitable for mild climates. Don't plant in cold districts or exposed gardens. Shelter is essential. Particularly good in mild, sheltered, coastal gardens. Does well in both sun and semi-shade. Any light to medium well-drained soil of average fertility will suffice. Be prepared to mulch generously on very light soils. Chalk is tolerated. Clip and prune during spring and summer. Avoid hard pruning – much better to cut or clip little and often.

Propagation Take semi-ripe wood cuttings in summer and root in warmth at 60–65°F (16–18°C).

POTENTILLA (POTENTILLA)

Recommended *Potentilla fruticosa* and varieties
Use For topiary sculptures and hedging. Best planted direct, but also good in containers.
Description Popular medium to slow-growing deciduous shrubs with mid-green cinquefoil leaves. Masses of flowers are produced all summer long in shades of yellow, orange, red or white. Ht and Sp variable, up to 5ft (1.5m), depending on variety.
Treatment Best in full sun, but, provided the garden is not too exposed, useful too for east or west aspects. Suitable for most areas. Thrives on light to medium well-drained soil of average fertility – good on chalk. Avoid over-rich soil and over-feeding. Clip regularly during summer, but not too severely or flowering will suffer.
Propagation Semi-ripe wood heel cuttings taken during August and September root well under a cold frame.

PRUNUS (CHERRY, PLUM, PEACH AND LAUREL)

Recommended Varieties of *Prunus cerasifera* (plum)
Varieties of *Prunus laurocerasus* (laurel)
Varieties of *Prunus persica* (peach)
Varieties of *Prunus serrulata* (Japanese cherry)
Uses Plum for topiary standards, hedging, arches and pleaching, and for pinch and prune pyramids. Cherry and plum for pinch and prune standards, festoons and Bonsai. Cherry, peach and plum for fans. Laurel for espaliers. Plant direct, Bonsai excepted.

Description Cherry, peach and plum are attractive quick-growing deciduous trees with pink and white spring flowers and red and yellow summer fruits. Laurel is an evergreen shrub grown for its glossy green leaves. Ht and Sp up to 18ft (5m).

Treatment Best in sun, except laurel, which does well in shade. Plum and laurel are suitable for most areas, but peach and cherry really need a mild climate. Any reasonable, well-limed, free-draining soil will do. Use bottom-worked plum and cherry for Bonsai. Clip or prune in summer.

Propagation Buy commercially-budded cherry, plum and peach varieties. Semi-ripe wood laurel cuttings taken in September should root well under a cold frame.

PYRACANTHA (FIRETHORN)

Recommended *Pyracantha atalantioides*

Use For topiary sculptures, arches, pleaching and wall forms, and for pinch and prune standards, spindle bushes, treillage and Bonsai. Best planted direct, Bonsai excepted.

Description Evergreen shrub grown for its white summer flowers and massed red autumn berries. Ht to 12ft (3.5m), Sp to 10ft (3m).

Treatment Best in sun, but adapts well to semi-shade. Suitable for most areas, but avoid east and north aspects in cold northern gardens. Any reasonable soil will do – good in chalk. Look for fireblight – promptly cut out and burn any affected shoots. Start clipping and pruning in summer after flowering.

Propagation Take semi-ripe wood cuttings in summer and root in warmth at 60°F (16°C). Or sow in autumn under a cold frame.

PYRUS (PEAR)

Recommended Varieties of *Pyrus communis*
      Pyrus salicifolia 'Pendula'

Use Varieties of *P. communis* for pinch and prune standards, cordons, espaliers, fans and Bonsai. Use 'Pendula' for weeping standards. All are suitable for spindle bushes. Plant direct.

Description Varieties of *P. communis* make attractive trees with white spring blossoms and a bonus of pear fruits. 'Pendula' is noted for its grey foliage and weeping habit. Ht 10–18ft (3–5m), Sp 8–15ft (2.5–4.5m).

Treatment Really needs sun. If planted in partial shade, set against a west wall. Hardy in most areas but will only reliably set fruit in milder districts devoid of late spring frosts. Above average soil is called for – chalky soils present no problems. Summer prune Bonsai and wall forms. Autumn prune standards.

Propagation Buy in commercially-budded or grafted stock. Bonsai plants can be raised by sowing seed in spring or summer.

RHODODENDRON (AZALEAS AND RHODODEN-DRONS)

Recommended Rhododendron hybrids, dwarf varieties included. Small-leaved varieties only.

Use For topiary hedging and pinch and prune standards and Bonsai. Good both in containers and planted *in situ*.

Description Colourful deciduous and evergreen shrubs; slow-growing. Spring flowering in shades of pink, red, orange, gold, blue and purple. Ht and Sp 1–6ft (30cm–1.8m).

Treatment Does well in sun and semi-shade. Best given a sheltered site. Avoid planting in north and east-facing aspects. Select hardy kinds for cold gardens. Acid, peaty or leafy, moist but free-draining soil is needed. *Do not plant on chalky soil.* Spray over the foliage of young plants in hot weather – using rain water for spraying and watering in hard water districts. Mulch young plants generously. Minimal pruning is required, otherwise you

risk forfeiting flowering for the following year.
Propagation Buy in initially. Subsequently, pin down layers in spring.

RHUS (SUMACH)

Recommended *Rhus typhina* and varieties
Use For pinch and prune standards. Best planted direct but will adapt to container growing.
Description Noteworthy deciduous shrubs/ trees with brilliant crimson and gold autumn tints. Ht and Sp to 10ft (3m).
Treatment Suitable for sun and semi-shade. Best in a mild, low rainfall area, sheltered from cold winds, and on average light to medium well-drained soil. Chalk tolerant. Excess feed and water diminishes autumn colouring. Prune in autumn or spring.
Propagation Rooted suckers detached in autumn or spring will grow away quite successfully.

RIBES (FLOWERING CURRANT)

Recommended *Ribes sanguineum* varieties
Ribes speciosum
Use For topiary hedging, and for pinch and prune standards and wall treillage. Best planted *in situ* – grow in containers if there is no alternative.
Description Reliable, easy and popular quick-growing deciduous shrubs. Pink and red spring flowers, followed by blue-black berries. Ht up to 7ft (2m), Sp up to 5ft (1.5m).
Treatment Best in semi-shade – does well on a west wall – but is also good in sun. Hardy in most areas (*R. speciosum* excepted – best reserved for milder sites). Average, reasonably fertile, moist soil is needed. Chalk tolerated. Prune in autumn.
Propagation Take hardwood cuttings in autumn and root outdoors.

ROSA (ROSE)

Recommended *Rosa various* – climber, rambler and bush, including both large- and cluster-flowered varieties.
Use For pinch and prune standards, weeping standards and wall treillage, plus Bonsai and miniatures. Best planted direct; smaller varieties satisfactory in containers.
Description Highly popular, quick-growing deciduous shrubs with a long flowering season from summer to autumn in a wide colour range. Ht up to 10ft (3m), Sp up to 12ft (3.5m).
Treatment Suitable for sunny and partially-shaded sites – a west aspect is best. Hardy in most areas, but give shelter in cold, exposed gardens. Soil of above average fertility is needed – don't plant on light, shallow, dry or chalky soils. Adhere to a rigid, regular spray programme to control pests and diseases, and feed generously. Permanent supports are necessary. Prune from spring to early autumn.
Propagation Take hardwood cuttings of climbers, ramblers and miniatures in autumn and root outdoors or under a frame. With regard to the others – buy in commercially-budded stock.

ROSMARINUS (ROSEMARY)

Recommended *Rosmarinus officinalis* and varieties
Use For topiary hedging and edging. Good in containers and planted direct.
Description Evergreen moderate to quick-growing shrub with aromatic grey-green foliage and blue spring/early summer flowers. Ht and Sp up to 5ft (1.5m).
Treatment A shrub best reserved for mild, sunny areas, and for average to light, free-draining, dryish soil. Good also on chalk. Clip regularly in summer and avoid cutting into hard old wood.

Propagation Semi-ripe wood heel cuttings taken in summer root well under cover. Hardwood cuttings taken in autumn are rooted outdoors.

SALIX (WILLOW)

Recommended *Salix caprea* 'Kilmarnock'
Use For pinch and prune standards. Best planted direct, unless in close proximity to a building, drains or services, when it is wise to containerise to avoid possible damage from invasive roots.
Description A deciduous, moderately quick-growing tree, noted for its weeping habit. Attractive silvery and yellow spring catkins and silvery summer foliage. Ht and Sp up to 8ft (2.5m).
Treatment Does well in sun and semi-shade. Hardy in most areas, provided shelter is given in exposed gardens. Any reasonable moist to very moist soil will do, provided it is not waterlogged. Good on chalky soil. Use a wire rose-trainer frame and tie in young branches to ensure an even spread of framework. Prune in autumn or spring.
Propagation Buy in budded or grafted stock.

SALVIA (SAGE)

Recommended Varieties of *Salvia officinalis*
Use For topiary edgings. Good when both direct-planted and grown in containers.
Description Moderate to slow-growing dwarf evergreen shrub, grown mainly for its aromatic foliage. The leaves are variegated grey, green and gold – sometimes tinged with purple. Ht 2ft (60cm), Sp 2½ft (75cm).
Treatment Best in full sun, but eminently suitable for west-facing positions. Thrives in a warm, mild climate, but will adapt to cooler areas, provided it is sheltered and in full sun. Sage must have free-draining soil, and is at its best on light to medium loam of average to low fertility. Good on chalk. Avoid planting on over-rich soil and don't over-feed. Clip during late spring and summer.
Propagation Take semi-ripe wood heel cuttings in September and root them under a cold frame.

SAMBUCUS (GOLDEN CUT-LEAF ELDER)

Recommended *Sambucus racemosa* 'Plumosa Aurea'
Use For pinch and prune standards. Suitable for direct planting or growing in containers.
Description A choice and spectacular moderate to quick-growing deciduous tree or shrub. The leaves are pleasing bright gold which sets off to good advantage the clusters of white summer flowers, and the red berries which follow. Ht up to 13ft (4m), Sp up to 10ft (3m).
Treatment In warm southern districts grow in partial shade, otherwise sun scorch can be a problem. In cold areas it does well in sun, provided it is given a sheltered position. Thrives in soil of average to rich fertility, and will stand chalk. Use strong potting compost in containers. A moist root run is preferred, so mulch young plants generously. Prune during autumn or winter.
Propagation Take semi-ripe wood cuttings in summer and root under a cold frame. Alternatively, take hardwood cuttings in autumn, again rooted under a cold frame, or even in a sheltered spot outdoors.
Note Not readily available, but well worth the trouble of looking out.

SANTOLINA (COTTON LAVENDER)

Recommended *Santolina chamaecyparissus* and varieties
Use For topiary edgings. Good planted *in situ* and in containers.

Description Attractive, feathery, quick-growing evergreen shrubs, grown mainly for their silvery grey or green foliage. The yellow button-like summer flowers are of secondary importance. Ht to 2ft (60cm); Sp to 2½ft (75cm).

Treatment Best in sun but adapts well to dappled shade. Hardy in most areas – cut hard back if frosted in a severe winter. Although light soil is preferred, any average soil will suffice. Don't spray overhead – you risk rotting foliage. Correct the natural tendency to grow wide tops and narrow bottoms by clipping regularly in summer – each month for a close-clipped effect. By so doing the flowers are sacrificed.

Propagation Root semi-ripe wood cuttings in a cold frame or on an indoor window-sill during summer.

SORBUS (MOUNTAIN ASH)

Recommended *Sorbus aucuparia* and
varieties
Sorbus reducta

Use *S. aucuparia* and varieties for pinch and prune standards, pyramids and spindle bushes. Reserve *S. reducta* for Bonsai only. Plant direct or in containers.

Description Deciduous trees/shrubs with white summer flowers followed by masses of red berries, with red and gold autumn leaf tints. Ht to 20ft (6m), Sp to 18ft (5m).

Treatment Grow in sun or semi-shade. Hardy in most areas but benefits from shelter in very exposed gardens. Any reasonably fertile soil is adequate. Makes satisfactory growth overlying chalk, provided the topsoil is at least 18in (45cm) deep. Once established tolerant of dryish as well as very moist conditions. Autumn prune standards, pyramids and spindle bushes. Spring and summer prune Bonsai.

Propagation Best to buy in budded or grafted stock. *S. aucuparia* and *S. reducta* can be raised for Bonsai by sowing seed in a cold frame in autumn.

SPIRAEA (SPIRAEA, BRIDAL WREATH)

Recommended *Spiraea x arguta*

Use For topiary hedging and for pinch and prune sculptures.

Description A medium to quick-growing deciduous shrub with arching branches and pleasing soft green leaves. Tiny white spring flowers are freely produced. Ht up to 7ft (2m), Sp up to 5ft (1.5m).

Treatment Suitable for both sun and semi-shade. Although spiraea adapts well to most areas it dislikes extremes of cold or exposure. Medium free-draining loam of average fertility is adequate, leafy soil the ideal. Clip during summer or early autumn, and when training sculptures, try to preserve the natural arching or weeping tendency of the branches.

Propagation Semi-ripe wood heel cuttings taken in summer root well under a cold frame. Hardwood cuttings taken in autumn will root under a cold frame or in a warm, sheltered spot outdoors.

SYRINGA (LILAC)

Recommended Varieties of *Syringa vulgaris*
Syringa microphylla 'Super-
ba'

Use All for pinch and prune standards, but only use *S. microphylla* for Bonsai. Grow direct-planted or in containers.

Description Much-loved deciduous, slow to moderately quick-growing, trees and shrubs. Blue, pink, carmine, purple and white (mainly spring flowering varieties) are available. Ht 5–10ft (1.5–3m), Sp 3½–10ft (1–3m).

Treatment Choose a sunny spot. Best in mild climates. Any reasonably moist soil will do – does well in heavy, chalky soil. Remove suckers on sight, dead-head young plants and de-blossom in the first year after planting to reduce the strain. Summer and autumn prune standards. Spring and summer prune Bonsai.

Propagation Buy in standards as grafted stock. Semi-ripe wood cuttings of *S. micro-phylla*, taken in summer and then rooted under a cold frame are most suitable for Bonsai.

TILIA (LIME)

Recommended *Tilia platyphyllos* and varieties

Use For topiary pleaching, and for pinch and prune standards. Plant direct, but containerise if essential to grow in close proximity to buildings and underground services.

Description A quick-growing deciduous tree, grown primarily for its soft green summer foliage and sweet-scented yellowish green summer flowers. The reddish-brown winter twigs are not unattractive. Ht up to 30ft (9m), Sp up to 15ft (4.5m).

Treatment Grows well in both sun and semi-shade. Best reserved for mild areas but worth a try elsewhere. Any average, reasonably fertile, free-draining soil will do. Tolerant of chalk. Avoid planting where extremes of wet or dry conditions are likely. Clip in summer, prune in autumn. Carry out any major pruning or shaping in autumn, *never* in spring when bleeding is a risk.

Propagation Best to buy in commercially-raised stock but layering in autumn is possible.

VIBURNUM (LAURUSTINUS)

Recommended *Viburnum tinus* and varieties

Use For pinch and prune standards. Best planted direct, but will adapt to container growing.

Description An attractive moderate to slow-growing evergreen shrub, noted for its flowers. *V. tinus* has white flowers and *V. tinus* 'Gwenllian' has blush-pink flowers. Occasionally, blue berries will follow the flowers. Ht and Sp up to 10ft (3m).

Treatment Suitable for both sunny and semi-shaded sites, and for most areas, except the very coldest. However, it does need shelter from freezing east and north winds in cold districts. Any reasonable well-drained soil will do – nothing too rich. Don't plant on excessively dry land. Use standard soil-based potting compost in containers. Prune during spring and summer.

Propagation Take semi-ripe wood cuttings in summer. Root under a cold frame, or in warmth at 60°F (16°C).

Note Immediately after heavy falls of snow, shake the crowns, otherwise there is a risk of branch breakages.

VITIS (VINE)

Recommended Varieties of *Vitis vinifera*

Use As wall treillage. Direct planting is best, but will grow reasonably well in containers.

Description Popular quick-growing deciduous climbers, grown mainly for their foliage. The crimson, orange, purple and pink autumn leaf tints are outstanding. Some varieties crop typical black grapes. Ht up to 25ft (7.5m), Sp up to 20ft (6m).

Treatment Grow in sun or on a west-facing aspect. Colours are richer in warm, sheltered, mild districts, but worthwhile in most areas. Soil of above average fertility is called for. Provided the topsoil is deep some underlying chalk is tolerated. Ensure a moist root run by generous mulching. Permanent supports are necessary. Avoid cutting in late winter or early spring, when bleeding is a risk. Prune in summer and autumn.

Propagation Ripe wood cuttings taken in autumn should be rooted in a frame.

WISTERIA (WISTERIA)

Recommended *Wisteria sinensis* and varieties

Use For pinch and prune standards and treillage. Plant direct or grow in containers.

Description A medium to quick-growing deciduous climber. The scented pendulous lavender, mauve and white late spring/early summer flowers are oustanding. Ht and Sp up to 20ft (6m) and more.

Treatment Reserve for sunny, mild climates. Soil of average fertility will suffice, but avoid excess lime and extremes of wet or dry. Spray newly set-out plants during their first year in hot weather. Summer prune laterals in July. Winter prune in February.

Propagation Best to buy in grafted standards. Semi-ripe wood heel cuttings taken in summer root reasonably well indoors in warmth at 60–65°F (16–18°C). Layers can be pinned down successfully in autumn.

IV   HARDY CONIFERS

CHAMAECYPARIS (FALSE CYPRESS)

Recommended *Chamaecyparis lawsoniana* and varieties.

Use For topiary sculptures, hedging and miniatures, and for pinch and prune Bonsai. Excellent both direct-planted and in containers.

Description Variety is all-important, ranging from dwarf slow growers to quick-growing medium-sized trees. Foliage in shades of green, blue and gold. Ht 12in–30ft (30cm–9m), Sp 12in to 10ft (30cm–3m).

Treatment Always buy container-grown stock. Grow in sun or semi-shade – most blue and gold varieties do best in sun. Hardy in most areas, but protect all plants for wind during their first winter and provide permanent shelter from east and north winds in cold, exposed gardens. Any average, reasonably fertile soil will suffice, chalky included. Avoid extremes of wet and dry; keep well watered in first spring and summer, spray over foliage in hot dry weather and mulch generously. Never cut back into hard wood. Clip in late spring and summer – prune Bonsai throughout early spring and summer.

Propagation Although semi-ripe wood cuttings taken in autumn will root under a frame or in warmth, the best policy is to buy in.

CUPRESSUS (CYPRESS)

Recommended *Cupressus macrocarpa*, plus the variety 'Gold Crest'

Use As *Chamaecyparis*.

Description Quick-growing evergreen trees with green or gold foliage. Ht to 18ft (5m), Sp to 13ft (4m).

Treatment Only for mild districts – suited to the coast and does best in sun. Avoid planting near to buildings, services and drains. Otherwise, treat as *Chamaecyparis*.

JUNIPERUS (JUNIPER)

Recommended *Juniperus communis* and varieties

Use As for *Chamaecyparis*

Description Slow-growing dwarf to medium-sized trees with aromatic foliage in greens, blues, silvers and golds. Variety very important, due to the large range of shapes from prostrate to pyramidal. Ht 12in to 10ft (30cm–3m), Sp 8in to 4ft (20cm–1.2m).

Treatment Best in sun but green foliage varieties good in semi-shade. Likes chalk. Treat as *Chamaecyparis*.

TAXUS (YEW)

Recommended *Taxus baccata* and varieties
Use For topiary sculptures, hedging, arches and wall topiary, and for pinch and prune standards and Bonsai. One of the very best. Excellent *in situ* and in containers.
Description Long-lived, slow to moderate-growing aromatic evergreens ranging from bushy to columnar in shape. Colourings from greens to silver variegated, with red arils (fruits). Ht and Sp up to 15ft (4.5m).
Treatment Does well in sun or semi-shade. Very hardy but provide shelter for variegated varieties in cold exposed gardens and always protect newly set-out plants from winter winds. Chalky soil preferred, but any reasonably fertile soil will do. Once established, dryish soils are tolerated. Always opt for container-raised plants. Poisonous to grazing animals – don't allow children to play with the fruits. Clip and prune in late spring and summer. Prune Bonsai throughout from early spring to late summer.
Propagation Semi-ripe wood cuttings taken in September will root under a cold frame, but plants are best bought in.

THUJA (ARBOR-VITAE)

Recommended *Thuja occidentalis* and varieties
Use For topiary hedging and simple sculptures, and for pinch and prune Bonsai. Suitable for containers and direct planting.
Description Range from slow-growing dwarf to moderately quick-growing medium sized. Plain green or silver/gold variegated evergreens are available. Ht 12in–10ft (30cm–3m), Sp 12in–4ft (30cm–1.2m).
Treatment Not quite as hardy as *Chamaecyparis*. Otherwise, can be treated similarly. Root cuttings in a cold frame, not in warmth.

V HARDY PERENNIAL PLANTS

ACAENA (BURR)

Recommended *Acaena microphylla*
Use For carpet bedding features in containers and beds.
Description Mound-forming, slow to moderate-growing carpet plants with tiny, ferny bronzy leaves and massed scarlet summer burrs. Ht to 2in (5cm), Sp to 20in (50cm).
Treatment Needs sun and shelter and is at its best in a warm summer. Any reasonable well-drained soil will do – avoid excess moisture. Move under a cold frame in autumn and plant outdoors in late spring. Clip over in summer.
Propagation Divide in autumn or spring.

ANTENNARIA (CAT'S EAR)

Recommended *Antennaria dioica* 'Rubra'
Use As *Acaena*.
Description Grey-leaved slow to moderately quick-growing carpeting plants with pink or white flowers in late spring and summer. Ht 2–4in (5–10cm), Sp up to 20in (50cm).
Treatment Suitable for most areas, provided it is given a sunny site. Clip off dead flower heads and trim to shape – otherwise, treat as *Acaena*.
Propagation Divide in spring.

AUBRIETA (AUBRIETA)

Recommended Varieties of *Aubrieta deltoides*
Use In carpet bed sculptures for an easy, reliable and tolerant beginner's plant. Foliage effects are good and it is excellent in containers.
Description A popular, evergreen perennial,

grown widely as rock plant. It is mound-forming with grey-green leaves. Scented blue, mauve, carmine or pink flowers are freely produced during spring. Ht 3–4in (8–10cm), Sp to 18in (45cm).

Treatment Best in sun, but quite satisfactory in partial shade. Suitable for most areas. Use standard soil-based potting compost, nothing too rich. Don't over-water. Clip over as necessary during spring and summer to keep plants neat and compact – don't worry unduly about the flowers, it is the dense-textured foliage which is important for carpet bed sculptures.

Overwintering Overwinter potted plants in a well-ventilated frame in cold areas. In mild areas they will be fine plunged outdoors in a sheltered spot.

Propagation Raise from seed sown indoors in warmth in spring, or in a cold frame. Alternatively, take softwood cuttings in summer and root under a cold frame, or divide up large clumps when repotting in autumn. Keep up a succession of young plants for the best carpet bed sculptures, discarding old plants after two or three years.

LYSIMACHIA (CREEPING JENNY)

Recommended *Lysimachia nummularia* and *L. n. 'Aurea'*

Use As *Acaena*.

Description Quick-growing, creeping or trailing evergreen plants, with small yellow summer flowers. Leaves green or yellowish green. Ht 2in (5cm), Sp to 20in (50cm).

Treatment Does well in sun and semi-shade. Suitable for most areas provided it is given a sheltered spot. Plant in well-worked soil of average fertility. Although a moisture-retentive soil is preferred, will stand temporary summer dryness. Move under a cold frame in autumn and plant outdoors in spring. Split up clumps in alternate years to

rejuvenate. Clip regularly to shape during spring and summer.

Propagation Divide in autumn or spring. Take softwood cuttings in spring.

MINUARTIA (ALSINE, SANDWORT)

Recommended *Minuartia verna caespitosa* 'Aurea'

Use As *Acaena*.

Description Moss, medium to slow-growing mat-forming plants with golden foliage and tiny white summer flowers. Ht 1in (3cm), Sp to 8in (20cm) and more.

Treatment Does best in sun. Suitable for most areas, provided shelter is given from drying winds. Light, chalky, well-drained, dryish soil is preferred, but any reasonable soil of average fertility will do. Move under a cold frame in autumn and plant out in spring. Divide annually or every two years to rejuvenate. Clip off dead flower heads and trim to shape.

Propagation Divide in spring.

SAXIFRAGA (SAXIFRAGE)

Recommended *Saxifraga* – mossy type

Use As *Acaena*.

Description Hummock or mat-forming medium to slow-growing evergreen mossy plants, smothered in pink, red, white or yellow flowers in spring. Ht 3–6in (8–15cm), Sp to 12in (30cm).

Treatment Does best in semi-shade but worthwhile in sun. Suitable for most areas. Any medium soil of average fertility will suffice. Move under a cold frame in autumn and plant outdoors in spring. Clip off dead flower heads and trim to shape throughout summer.

Propagation Divide in spring.

SEDUM (STONECROP)

Recommended *Sedum spathulifolium* 'Cape Blanco'
Use As *Acaena*.
Description Evergreen, grey-leaved medium to slow-growing mound-forming plants covered with yellow flowers in summer. Ht 4in (10cm), Sp to 10in (25cm).
Treatment Plant in a sunny spot. Does best in warm districts. Thrives in light to medium dryish soil of average fertility. Don't spray overhead or risk rotting. Move under a cold frame in autumn and plant outdoors in spring. Clip over to dead-head.
Propagation Take offsets or divide in autumn or spring. Alternatively take softwood cuttings in spring and summer and root in a cold frame, or take leaf cuttings. It is vital that a constant succession of young plants should be kept up.

SEMPERVIVUM (HOUSE LEEK)

Recommended *Sempervivum schlehanii* 'Rubrifolium'
Use As *Acaena*.
Description Slow-growing rosette-forming plant with flesh-red, persistent leaves. Ht 4–6in (10–15cm), Sp 4in (10cm) and more.
Treatment Treat in a similar manner to *sedum*, but cut off flower spikes on sight.
Propagation Tease away and pot up rooted offsets in autumn or spring.

VI HALF-HARDY PLANTS

ABUTILON (FLOWERING MAPLE)

Recommended *Abutilon megapotamicum* and varieties
Use For pinch and prune standards and pyramids, and for wall-trained espaliers and fans plus treillage. Suitable for both containers and *in situ* planting.
Description Medium to slow-growing semi-evergreen shrub with lantern-like orange-red and yellow flowers all summer. Ht up to 7ft (2m), Sp up to 4ft (1.2m).
Treatment Does best in sun, in a sheltered garden in a mild area. *Not* for cold exposed sites. Average to moderately rich, fertile soil is needed for best results. Prune during summer and autumn.
Overwintering Outdoors *in situ*, provided against a warm wall. Otherwise, move into an unheated or cool greenhouse.
Propagation Take semi-ripe cuttings in summer and root indoors at 60°F (16°C). Renew plants every three to four years.

ALTERNANTHERA (JOY-WEED)

Recommended *Alternanthera amoena* and varieties
Use For carpet bed sculptures – excellent in containers.
Description Tender dwarf sub-tropical perennials, grown for their brilliant pink, red and crimson foliage. Ht 4in (10cm), Sp up to 8in (20cm).
Treatment Needs a sunny, sheltered spot, and is only really suitable for warm, mild climates. Don't use in cold areas or in exposed gardens. Use soil-based standard potting compost, and keep it uniformly moist. It is important to avoid extremes of wet and dry during the growing season. Plants are kept barely moist during winter. Don't plant outdoors before June – plants should be returned indoors by mid-September at the latest. Clip over plants regularly throughout summer.
Overwintering Pot or box up and overwinter in warmth at 55–60°F (13–16°C).
Propagation Take softwood basal cuttings in spring and root at 60–65°F (16–18°C).

ARDISIA (CORAL BERRY)

Recommended *Ardisia crispa*
Use For pinch and prune standards. Grow in containers for indoor use.
Description A tender, slow-growing un-common evergreen shrub with attractive leathery mid-green leaves. Grown mainly for its bright red winter berries which follow on well after the white June flowers. Ht up to 3ft (90cm), Sp up to 2ft (60cm).
Treatment Coral berry is only really suited for greenhouse or conservatory growing. Shade lightly in late spring and summer and give maximum light at other times of year. Use standard soil-based potting compost. Water moderately in summer, but only sparingly in winter. Pinch and prune during spring and summer.
Overwintering Indoors in cool conditions at 45–50°F (7–10°C).
Propagation Take semi-ripe wood heel cuttings in summer and root in warmth at 60–65°F (16–18°C).
Note Although it is not readily available it is well worth looking out. It is very slow-growing but long-lived – expect it to last 20 years and longer.

BELOPERONE (SHRIMP PLANT)

Recommended *Beloperone guttata*
Use For pinch and prune semi-weeping standards. Grow in containers for greenhouse or conservatory display, or as a house plant.
Description A tender, moderate to slow-growing evergreen sun-shrub, grown for its curious, flower-like, pendulous, pinkish-brown bracts which appear in succession all sum-mer long. Ht up to 3ft (90cm), Sp up to 2ft (60cm).
Treatment Shade lightly in spring and summer. Grow in well-lit, airy conditions under cover where the temperature is not going to rise above 70°F (21°C). Use standard soil-based potting compost. Water moder-ately in summer, misting over the foliage daily. Keep on the dryish side in winter. Permanent supports are needed. Pinching and pruning is mainly carried out during spring and summer.
Overwintering Indoors at 45–50°F (7–10°C).
Propagation Take semi-ripe wood cuttings in spring or summer and root in warmth at 60–65°F (16–18°C).

BOUGAINVILLEA (BOUGAINVILLEA)

Recommended Varieties of *Bougainvillea × buttiana*
Use For pinch and prune standards and treillage. Grow and display indoors in pots.
Description These tender, moderate to quick-growing deciduous climbers are grown for their massed bright pink, red or orange summer bracts. Ht up to 8ft (2.5m), Sp up to 3½ft (1m) (when roots are restricted to a container).
Treatment Bougainvillea is only really suited to growing in a warm greenhouse or conservatory where a temperature of 55–70°F (13–21°C) can be maintained. Ensure well-lit conditions, shading lightly during summer. Use standard soil-based potting compost. Water freely in summer, when they also need high humidity – mist over and damp down daily. Keep barely moist during winter, withholding water gradually as the leaves begin to fall. Permanent supports are needed. Pinch and prune during spring and summer.
Overwintering Indoors where a tem-perature around 50°F (10°C) can be main-tained.
Propagation Take semi-ripe wood heel cuttings in summer and root in warmth at 65–70°F (18–21°C).
Note These plants are difficult to grow in the home as house plants.

CAREX (SEDGE)

Recommended *Carex morrowii* 'Evergold'
Use Topiary edging and carpet bed sculptures. Plant direct or in containers.
Description A medium to slow-growing, tuft- or clump-forming, evergreen dwarf, grass-like sedge with narrow, gold, variegated leaves. Marginally hardy. Ht and Sp 6–10in (15–25cm).
Treatment Given a sheltered spot, grows well in sun or semi-shade. *Not* for cold, exposed gardens. Soil of average fertility is suitable. Stands chalk and a moist root run. Good for water-side plantings. Cut off flower stalks, don't allow to self-seed. Clip over to shape in late summer or spring.
Overwintering Move under the cover of a cold frame or cool greenhouse before autumn frosts. It is important to protect from frost at all times. Move outdoors in late spring.
Propagation Divide in spring – aim to replace plants every two to three years.

CARISSA (NATAL PLUM)

Recommended *Carissa grandiflora*
Use For pinch and prune standards, pyramids and Bonsai. Grow in containers and display indoors.
Description A tender medium to slow-growing prickly evergreen shrub, grown for its fragrant white summer flowers, and for its reddish, edible, sweet plum-like late summer fruits. Ht and Sp up to 5ft (1.5m).
Treatment Only suitable for growing in a warm greenhouse or conservatory, or as a house plant. Keep well-lit year round, but shade lightly during summer. Use standard soil-based potting compost. Keep moist throughout the year. It is important to water freely during summer while flowering and fruiting. Pinch and prune during spring and summer, pinching in the sides regularly to counteract the tendency of this shrub to a wide spreading habit.
Overwintering Indoors at 50–55°F (10–13°C).
Propagation Take semi-ripe wood heel cuttings during summer and root in warmth at 65–70°F (18–21°C).

CHRYSANTHEMUM (MARGUERITE)

Recommended *Chrysanthemum frutescens* and varieties.
Use For pinch and prune standards. Grow in containers.
Description A bushy, tender sub-shrub with glaucous blue-green leaves and large daisy-like white or gold flowers all summer long and into autumn. Ht and Sp up to 3½ft (1m).
Treatment During summer, stand containers in a sheltered spot in sun or semi-shade. A good plant for mild districts – better grown on in a cold greenhouse or conservatory in cold districts. Use strong soil-based potting compost. Keep well watered in spring and summer, and slightly moist during winter. Provide permanent supports. Stop plants when they reach 18in–2ft (45–60cm). Pinch to form a bushy crown throughout the season. Dead-head promptly. Plants are discarded after a full season's flowering.
Overwintering Move into a cool or intermediate greenhouse.
Propagation Softwood cuttings taken in spring or summer are rooted at 55°F (13°C) then grown on steadily at 50°F (10°C).

COLEUS (FLAME NETTLE)

Recommended Varieties of *Coleus blumei*
Use For pinch and prune standards and pyramids. Best grown in containers.
Description A brilliantly colourful foliage perennial with variegated and multi-coloured leaves in shades of green, red, orange, cream

and amber. Ht up to 4ft (1.2m), Sp up to 3ft (90cm).

Treatment In cold areas and exposed gardens, grow indoors year round, keeping semi-shaded during summer. Otherwise, in mild areas, choose a sunny, sheltered spot outdoors. Use strong soil-based potting compost. Permanent supports are needed. Water freely in summer, sparingly in winter. Old plants are discarded each autumn. Stop standards at 20in (50cm). Pinch and prune both standards and pyramids throughout the growing season.

Overwintering Indoors in warmth at 55–60°F (13–16°C) in sunny, well-lit positions – this refers to young, September-struck cuttings.

Propagation Take softwood cuttings in spring – make it early September for the tallest standards – root in warmth at 55°F (13°C).

ECHEVERIA (ECHEVERIA)

Recommended *Echeveria glauca*
Use For carpet bed sculptures. Normally displayed in containers.
Description A stemless, rosette-forming succulent. Slow-growing, grown mainly for its fleshy, blue-green leaves. The orange-yellow summer flowers are a bonus. Ht 3–6in (8–15cm), Sp 3in (8cm).
Treatment At its best in mild areas, in a sunny, sheltered spot, but it will stand some shade. Use standard soil-based potting compost. Keep dryish at the roots during the growing season and don't spray overhead. Keep barely moist during winter. Dead-head after flowering.
Overwintering Move indoors in autumn and overwinter in cool conditions at 45°F (7°C). Set out in late spring – don't allow to get frosted.
Propagation Remove offsets as they arise

during spring and summer and pot them up. Alternatively, take leaf cuttings.

EUPHORBIA (SCARLET PLUME)

Recommended *Euphorbia fulgens*
Use For pinch and prune weeping standards. Grow in containers and display indoors.
Description A spectacular, tender, quick to moderate-growing deciduous shrub with arching wand-like branches. During winter, brilliant scarlet flowers are massed along the branches. Ht up to 5ft (1.5m), Sp up to 4ft (1.2m).
Treatment Grow in a warm greenhouse or conservatory where a temperature of 60–70°F (16–21°C) can be maintained during the growing season. Good illumination is needed, but lightly shade from strong sun in spring and summer. Use strong, soil-based potting compost. Increase watering gradually in spring; water freely in summer. Decrease watering gradually in autumn, but be sure to keep moist until after flowering. After flowering, withhold water for three or four weeks. During summer increase humidity by misting over and damping down daily. Pinch and prune young plants during spring and summer. Prune mature plants annually after flowering.
Overwintering Maintain a minimum temperature of 55°F (13°C) up to and during flowering. Drop it back to 50°F (10°C) during the rest period.
Propagation Take semi-ripe wood cuttings in spring and root in warmth at 65–70°F (18–21°C). Dip cuttings in charcoal – this helps to dry off the milky sap on the cut surfaces which retards rooting. The milky sap is poisonous and can set up allergies.

FESTUCA (FESCUE)

Recommended *Festuca glauca*
Use For topiary carpet bed sculptures and edgings. Normally grown in containers, but can be useful planted direct.
Description A moderately quick-growing blue-green tuft- or clump-forming dwarf grass. Ht and Sp 6in (15cm).
Treatment Suitable for most areas – thrives in sun. Use standard soil-based potting compost. Clip to shape in late summer or spring.
Overwintering If planted direct as an edging, hardy enough to remain outdoors in mild areas. Otherwise, move under cover in early autumn, overwintering in unheated but frost-free conditions. Ventilate freely throughout the winter months without causing draughts, and keep on the dry side. Set outdoors in late spring.
Propagation Divide up clumps in spring, or sow seed in a cold frame in spring.

FICUS (FIG, CREEPING CHARLIE)

Recommended *Ficus pumila*
Use As pinch and prune multi-stemmed pyramids. Grow in containers.
Description A quick-growing trailing or climbing, evergreen tender perennial with green leaves and branching habit. Ht and Sp to 5ft (1.5m).
Treatment Best grown indoors year round in cool to intermediate temperatures. Don't allow the temperature to rise above 7°F (21°C) during summer. Keep lightly shaded in spring and summer. Once trained can be moved outdoors during summer in mild areas, into a favoured, sheltered spot out of wind and out of fierce midday sun. Use standard or strong soil-based potting compost. Keep well watered during spring and summer and mist over the leaves regularly.

Pinch side-shoots back every three weeks or so during the growing season. Provide permanent supports.
Overwintering Indoors at 50°F (10°C) minimum in a sunny, well-lit position, keeping on the dryish side.
Propagation Either take softwood cuttings in spring and summer, rooting them at 60°F (16°C), or pin down layers in spring.

FUCHSIA (LADIES' EAR DROPS)

Recommended Varieties of *Fuchsia hybrida* (choose the strong growers as the easiest and most satisfactory to train)
Use For pinch and prune standards and pyramids. Mostly grown in containers, but useful planted direct amongst summer bedding as dot plants.
Description Highly popular, quick-growing tender shrubs with pendulous pink, red, purple and white flowers. Some varieties have gold or silver variegated leaves. Ht up to 7ft (2m), Sp up to 4ft (1.2m). Variety is all-important.
Treatment Shade lightly indoors during spring and summer. Outdoors choose a sunny, mild sheltered spot, shaded from fierce midday sun. Use strong soil-based potting compost. Water freely and mist over in spring and summer. Keep drier during autumn and winter. Provide permanent supports. Pinch and prune during spring and summer.
Overwintering Young well-leafed rooted cuttings need to be overwintered at 55°F (13°C). Dormant, leafless mature standards and pyramids are overwintered at 40–45°F (5–7°C).
Propagation Take softwood cuttings in spring; make it August-September for the tallest standards and pyramids. Root all cuttings at 55°F (13°C). Expect to replace standards and pyramids every three to four years.

GLECHOMA (GROUND IVY)

Recommended *Glechoma hederacea* 'Variegata'

Use For pinch and prune multi-stemmed dwarf pyramids to display in the conservatory, or outdoors in summer. Grow in containers.

Description A moderate to slow-growing trailing or climbing herbaceous perennial with attractive silver-variegated, slightly aromatic leaves. Ht and Sp up to 2–3ft (60–90cm).

Treatment Ideally, stand the container in a sunny, south-facing position outdoors. But it will also do well given a west-facing aspect. In the conservatory, provide light shade during summer and don't allow temperatures to rise above 70°F (21°C). Provided plants are sheltered from wind they are suitable for most areas. Keep well-watered in summer, dryish at other times of the year and barely moist during winter. Pinch out side-shoots throughout spring and summer.

Overwintering Indoors in cool conditions at 45–50°F (7–10°C). Move plants outdoors in late May or early June and return them back indoors by mid-September.

Propagation Expect dwarf pyramids to last four or five years. Keep up a succession of young plants for replacement purposes. Increase is by division in autumn or spring.

HELIOTROPIUM (HELIOTROPE OR CHERRY PIE)

Recommended Varieties of *Heliotropium hybridum*

Use For pinch and prune standards, mainly grown in containers. Display indoors or on the patio. Useful planted direct as dot plants in summer bedding.

Description Tender medium to slow-growing evergreen shrubs, noted for their sweet-scented mauve, lavender or purple summer flowers. Ht to 2ft (60cm), Sp to 18in (45cm).

Treatment Indoors, shade lightly during spring and summer. Choose a sunny, mild favoured spot outdoors. Use strong soil-based potting compost. Water moderately in spring and summer, keep on the dry side in winter. Provide permanent supports. Pinch and prune throughout spring and summer, taking care not to knock off any of the brittle leaves accidentally.

Overwintering Young rooted cuttings should be overwintered at 60°F (16°C) – similarly with mature plants required to flower early. Otherwise 50°F (10°C) is adequate for mature plants, but flowering will be later.

Propagation Take softwood cuttings, preferably in late summer, alternatively in spring, to increase named varieties and others. Good plants can be raised from seed sown indoors in spring. Root or germinate at 65°F (18°C). Heliotrope standards need to be replaced every two to three years.

HERNIARIA (RUPTURE-WORT)

Recommended *Herniaria glabra*

Use For carpet bed sculptures and for edgings. Good in containers, and can be planted direct.

Description A moderate to slow-growing carpeting or trailing plant with ornamental bright green foliage. Ht 1in (3cm), Sp up to 10in (25cm) and more.

Treatment A tolerant plant which grows well in sun or shade. Rupture-wort is hardy in mild districts where it is at its best. However, in colder climes it is fine treated as a half-hardy plant, provided it is sheltered. Use standard soil-based potting compost – nothing too rich – or plant direct into any reasonable soil. Keep well-watered in summer and dryish in winter. Clip around the edges in spring and summer to keep plants tidy and in good shape.

Overwintering In cooler areas overwinter in

an unheated frame or frost-free greenhouse at 40–45°F (4–7°C). Set plants outdoors in spring in late May and return them under cover in September. In mild areas, plants which have been set out direct are overwintered outdoors.

Propagation Divide up clumps in autumn or spring. Keep up a succession of young plants – anything older than two or three years isn't really suitable for carpet bed sculptures.

IMPATIENS (BUZY LIZZIE)

Recommended Varieties of *Impatiens wallerana*

Use For pinch and prune carpet bed sculptures. Grow in containers.

Description Quick-growing herbaceous perennials with masses of pink, red, white, orange, mauve and bi-coloured flowers from spring to autumn. Ht and Sp 5–12in (13–30cm).

Treatment Suitable for most areas if sheltered from cold winds. Plant sculptures in a semi-shaded spot. Use standard potting compost. Plants are best disposed of after flowering but can be overwintered to provide more cuttings. Remove the growing point at the six-leaf stage, then pinch occasionally in spring and summer to make plants bushy. Dead-head to tidy.

Overwintering Young, later-summer-rooted cuttings are overwintered at 50°F (10°C).

Propagation Softwood cuttings will root readily from spring to autumn at 60°F (16°C). Good plants can be raised from seed sown early spring and germinated at 65–70°F (18–21°C). Plants are renewed annually.

IPOMOEA (MORNING GLORY)

Recommended *Ipomoea tricolor*

Use For pinch and prune multi-stemmed pyramids. Grow in containers and display as a conservatory feature, or on the patio, or plunge-planted in a favourite position.

Description Tender, quick-growing perennial climber, best treated as a half-hardy annual. Ht up to 10ft (3m), Sp up to 16in (40cm).

Treatment Only really suitable for outdoor growing in mild areas. Shade lightly indoors and position in a sunny, sheltered position outdoors. Use strong soil-based potting compost. Train 5 to 7 plants to a 10in (25cm) pot, pinching in spring and early summer.

Overwintering Not overwintered as a rule.

Propagation Sow seed annually each spring and germinate at 70°F (21°C). Pre-soak the seed for 4–6 hours in tepid water in a warm room before sowing.

JASMINUM (JASMINE)

Recommended *Jasminum polyanthum*
                Jasminum primulinum

Use For pinch and prune sculptures and multi-stemmed pyramids. Grow in containers for indoor or conservatory display.

Description Tender climbing plants with delicate pinnate foliage. *J. polyanthum* produces its white flower clusters in winter. *J. primulinum* (Syn. *J. mesnyi*) has yellow flowers in the spring. Ht 4–6ft (1.2–1.8m), Sp to 2ft (60cm).

Treatment Keep plants semi-shaded if summered indoors. In warm, mild climate areas the plants are best stood outdoors – in a sheltered south or west-facing spot. This ripens the wood and makes for more prolific flowering the following season. Use standard soil-based potting compost. Water freely during summer, sparingly in winter. Pinch and prune young plants to shape during summer. Prune mature plants after flowering, in spring or summer depending on variety. Jasmine needs permanent supports and must be tied in regularly.

Overwintering Indoors, maintaining a temperature of 50–55°F (10–13°C).
Propagation Take semi-ripe heal cuttings in September and root in warmth at 60–65°F (16–18°C). Alternatively, pin down layers in September or October.

LANTANA (LANTANA)

Recommended Varieties of *Lantana camara*
Use For pinch and prune standards. Best grown in containers for indoor and outdoor use. Display in the conservatory, on the patio, or plunge-planted as dot plants amidst summer bedding.
Description Tender, medium to slow-growing evergreen shrubs with scented summer flower clusters in combinations of red and yellow; rose and yellow; lilac and yellow and white and yellow. Ht to 4ft (1.2m), Sp to 3ft (90cm).
Treatment Outdoor growing best reserved for mild areas. Lightly shade indoors during summer. Position in a sheltered spot in full sun outdoors. Use strong potting compost. Stand containers on moist, pebble-filled containers during summer, and water moderately. Don't mist over the leaves, and water sparingly in winter. Provide permanent supports. Deadhead regularly and prune during spring and summer.
Overwintering Both young cuttings and mature plants are overwintered in warmth at 60°F (16°C).
Propagation Take softwood cuttings, ideally in late summer, but spring will do. Root at 65–70°F (18–21°C). Within two or three years reasonable plants can be raised from seed sown in spring and germinated at 65–70°F (18–21°C). Plants need to be renewed every five to seven years.

LOBELIA (LOBELIA)

Recommended Varieties of *Lobelia erinus*
Use For carpet bed sculptures and for edgings. Excellent both in containers and planted direct.
Description Although technically these are quick-growing, mound-forming, short-lived perennials, it is usual to treat them as half-hardy annuals. Blue, mauve, carmine or white flowers are produced in great profusion throughout summer. Ht 4in (10cm), Sp up to 8in (20cm).
Treatment At its best in sun, but in warm gardens semi-shade is fine. Suitable for most areas. Use standard soil-based potting compost or plant direct into any reasonable soil. Water freely throughout summer. Discard flowered plants in autumn and start afresh again in spring. Clip back any straggly growths during summer.
Propagation Sow seeds annually in late winter and germinate at 65°F (18°C). Prick out three or four seedlings together so that they will form dense clumps.

MANETTIA (FIRECRACKER)

Recommended *Manettia inflata*
Use For pinch and prune multi-stemmed pyramid. For container growing in a conservatory.
Description A moderately to quick-growing perennial climber with red and yellow flowers from spring to autumn. Ht up to 10ft (3m), Sp up to 18in (45cm).
Treatment Shade from strong midday summer sun, and don't allow the temperature to rise above 75°F (23°C). Use strong soil-based potting compost. Water freely and mist over leaves in summer – keep on the dry side in winter. Provide permanent supports and pinch and prune throughout summer.
Overwintering In warmth at 50°F (10°C).

Propagating Softwood cuttings taken in summer root well at 60–65°F (16–18°C). Replace plants every four to five years.

PASSIFLORA (PASSION FLOWER)

Recommended *Passiflora caerulea* and variety 'Constance Elliott'
Use For pinch and prune multi-stemmed pyramids, double cordons and wall treillage. Grown mainly indoors. Good in containers and direct-planted.
Description A tender, quick-growing evergreen climber with mid-green leaves. When grown outdoors in mild areas it is semi-evergreen. Noted for its blue and white, or white, summer flowers. Orange-yellow fruits follow in early autumn. Ht up to 13ft (4m), Sp up to 10ft (3m).
Treatment Indoor growing – shade lightly during late spring and summer, give sun at other times of year. Outdoor growing – choose a sunny or partially-shaded south- or west-facing sheltered position. Only attempt outdoor growing in mild areas. Use strong soil-based potting compost. Plant direct into rich, fertile soil. Water freely in summer, keep on the dryish side in winter. Pinch and prune young plants and mature in summer. Prune annually in spring. Provide permanent supports.
Overwintering In mild areas, outdoor direct-planted climbers must be given extra root protection. Otherwise, overwinter indoors at 45–50°F (7–10°C).
Propagation Take semi-ripe wood cuttings in summer and root at 60–65°F (16–18°C). Good plants can be raised from seed sown in spring and germinated at 65–75°F (18–21°C).

PELARGONIUM (GERANIUM)

Recommended Varieties of *Pelargonium x hortorum* – opt for the strongest growers

Use For pinch and prune standards and for indoor wall treillage. Best grown in containers. Display standards in a conservatory, on the patio or plunge-planted in summer bedding as dot plants.
Description Tender evergreen sub-shrubs, which bloom from spring to autumn in shades of pinks, red, scarlet, crimson, orange and white. Some have gold or white variegated foliage, others multi-coloured. Ht up to 5ft (1.5m), Sp up to 4ft (1.2m).
Treatment Ideal plants for mild areas, but worth trying in sheltered gardens, even in cold districts. Do best in sun, but indoors must be shaded from midday summer sun. Use strong potting compost. Water moderately in summer, and sparingly in winter. Provide permanent supports and pinch from spring through to autumn.
Overwintering Trained mature plants are overwintered at 50°F (10°C). Raise the temperatures to 55°F (13°C) for rooted cuttings and plants in the process of being trained into the tallest standards.
Propagation Root softwood cuttings in June/July for the tallest standards. Otherwise, August or spring is fine. Both standards and treillage need renewing every two or three years.

PERILLA (PERILLA)

Recommended *Perilla frutescens* and varieties
Use For pinch and prune softwood standards. Grow in containers whether growing for indoor specimens or for outdoor plunge-planting as dot plants amidst summer bedding.
Description Quick-growing annuals grown for their bold, big bronze, chocolate or purples leaves – mainly selfs but some bi-coloured. Ht up to 3½ft (1in), Sp up to 2½ft (75cm).

Treatment Shade lightly indoors. Outdoors choose a sunny south- or west-facing sheltered bed. Not for outdoor use in cold areas or exposed gardens. Use strong soil-based potting compost. Gradually increase watering as plants grow, watering freely when in full growth. Plants need supports throughout their lives. Pinch and prune from late winter to summer, and dispose of plants in autumn.

Propagation Raise from seed sown in September or late winter, and germinate at 65–70°F (18–21°C). Young seedling plants should be overwintered at 50–55°F (10–13°C).

PLUMBAGO (LEADWORT)

Recommended *Plumbago capensis*
Use For pinch and prune multi-stemmed standards, wall-trained cordons and indoor treillage. Good in containers for standards and cordons indoors or out. Plant direct into the greenhouse or conservatory border for treillage.
Description A moderate to quick-growing climbing evergreen, with a succession of blue flowers from spring through to late autumn. Ht up to 12ft (3.5m), Sp up to 18in (45cm).
Treatment Reserve for mild areas and sheltered gardens. Position containers in a sunny spot outdoors, but shade from strong midday summer sun indoors. Use strong soil-based potting compost. Water freely and mist during the flowering season; water sparingly in winter. Permanent supports are called for. Pinch in spring and summer, and prune in autumn after flowering.
Overwintering In cool conditions at 45°F (7°C).
Propagation Softwood cuttings taken in summer root at 55–60°F (13–16°C) with little trouble. Plants need to be renewed every three years or so.

PUNICA (POMEGRANATE)

Recommended *Punica granatum* 'Nana'
Use For pinch and prune standards and Bonsai. Grow in containers.
Description A tender moderate to slow-growing deciduous dwarf tree or shrub, grown mainly for its red summer flowers. Ht up to 3ft (90cm), Sp up to 2ft (60cm).
Treatment Stand outdoors during summer in mild areas and sheltered gardens; otherwise, grow indoors year round and don't allow the temperature to rise above 75°F (23°C). Needs a sunny spot – both indoors and out – but protect from strong midday sun. Use strong potting compost for standards, and Bonsai mix for Bonsai. Water freely in spring and summer, keep barely moist in winter. Pinch and prune from spring to autumn.
Overwintering Move indoors in September and overwinter at 45°F (7°C). Don't move these frost-sensitive plants outdoors before June.
Propagation Take semi-ripe wood cuttings in summer and root at 60–65°F (16–18°C). Standards need replacing every four or five years.

RHOICISSUS (GRAPE IVY)

Recommended *Rhoicissus rhomboidea*
Use As a pinch and prune multi-stemmed pyramid. Grow in containers for indoor display.
Description Quick-growing evergreen climber, renowned for its dark green leaves. Ht up to 7ft (2m), Sp up to 2ft (60cm) – when grown in containers, otherwise, much larger.
Treatment Position container in a well-lit, semi-shaded spot, and don't allow temperatures to rise above 65–70°F (18–21°C). Use standard soil-based potting compost. Water moderately from spring

through summer and mist over the leaves. Keep on the dry side during winter. Permanent supports are needed. Pinch from spring to autumn.

Overwintering Temperatures from 45–50°F (7–10°C) are about right.

Propagation Take softwood cuttings in summer and root at 60–65°F (16–18°C).

SAGINA (PEARLWORT)

Recommended *Sagina glabra* and *S.glabra* 'Aurea'

Use For carpet bed sculptures and grown in containers.

Description Slow-growing, mat-forming, green or golden grassy, mossy, hardy perennials. Although hardy, treat as half-hardy so as to maintain good colouring. Tiny white summer flowers as a bonus. Ht 1–2in (3–5cm), Sp 6in (15cm) plus.

Treatment Suitable for most areas. Position sculptures in a semi-shaded sheltered spot. Use standard potting compost and pot into seed trays or half pots. Don't use containers over 3in (8cm) deep or you will risk souring. Keep reasonably moist in summer – much drier in winter. Neaten back straggly edges in spring or autumn.

Overwintering Stand plants in a cold frame.

Propagation Divide clumps in spring or autumn, repotting only the outer young segments. Raise good plants from seed sown in trays under a cold frame in spring.

SCLERANTHUS (SCLERANTHUS)

Recommended *Scleranthus biflorus*

Use For carpet bed sculptures. Excellent in containers.

Description A slow-growing, ground-hugging perennial. Its fresh green foliage looks rather like grass in miniature. Ht 2in (5cm), Sp 4in (10cm).

Treatment Does well in both sun and semi-shade. Suitable for most areas, but avoid setting out in cold exposed sites. Use standard soil-based potting compost – nothing too rich. Aim to keep the roots moist but not over-wet, especially in winter. Clip throughout summer to keep tidy and compact.

Overwintering Pot or box up and overwinter under a cold frame or in a greenhouse, in frost-free conditions.

Propagation Divide up clumps in autumn as they are removed from the sculptures and potted or boxed up. Alternatively, divide up when setting out in spring. Keep up a succession of young plants – they need to be renewed regularly every two or three years.

SEDUM (STONECROP)

Recommended *Sedum sieboldii* 'Medio-variegatum'

Use For carpet bed sculptures. Best grown in containers.

Description A slow-growing evergreen perennial with attractive white, variegated, glaucous blue-green fleshy leaves. Ht 2–3in (5–8cm), Sp up to 15in (38cm).

Treatment In mild climates, position summer outdoor sculptures in a warm, sheltered, sunny south- or west-facing position. Not for cold districts or exposed gardens. Use standard soil-based or cactus potting compost. Keep plants moderately moist in summer and dryish in winter. Remove all flowers as they arise as they will discourage leaf growth, which is the main attraction.

Overwintering Indoors maintaining a temperature of 50–55°F (10–13°C). These are frost-tender plants, so don't set outdoors before June and move back indoors well before the autumn frosts.

Propagation Take softwood cuttings in spring or summer and root in warmth at 50–60°F (10–16°C).

SENECIO (SENECIO)

Recommended *Senecio macroglossus*
'Variegatus'
Senecio mikanoides
Use For pinch and prune indoor sculptures and treillage. Grow in containers.
Description Evergreen climbing or trailing plants. *S. mikanoides* has green leaves. *S. macroglossus* 'Variegata' is grown for its golden variegated foliage. Ht 3½ft–4ft (1–1.2m), Sp 2ft (60cm).
Treatment Position containers in good light. Shade from strong summer sun and don't allow temperatures to rise above 70°F (21°C). Use strong potting compost. Water moderately during summer and mist over the foliage regularly. Keep on the dry side in winter. Permanent supports are needed. Prune from spring through to autumn.
Overwintering Maintain temperatures at around 55°F (13°C).
Propagation Pin down layers in spring, or take softwood cuttings in summer and root at 60°F (16°C).

SOLEIROLIA (HELXINE, MIND-YOUR-OWN-BUSINESS)

Recommended *Soleirolia soleirolii* and varieties
Use For carpet bed sculptures. Grow in containers.
Description Evergreen, moderate to slow-growing carpeting perennials with green, gold or white variegated foliage. Ht 2–3in (5–8cm), Sp 6in (15cm) plus.
Treatment Suitable for most climates. Sculptures are grown outdoors during summer in semi-shaded sheltered spots. Use

standard soil-based potting compost. Water freely in summer and mist over regularly; keep somewhat drier in winter. Clip over occasionally to tidy from spring to autumn.
Overwintering Move plants under cover in autumn and overwinter at 45°F (7°C) – set outdoors in spring.
Propagation Divide up clumps in spring. Plants need renewing every two to three years.

STREPTOSOLEN (STREPTOSOLEN, MARMALADE PLANT)

Recommended *Streptosolen jamesonii*
Use For pinch and prune standards to display in the conservatory, or outdoors on the patio, or plunge-planted as a dot plant amidst summer bedding. Also attractive as indoor treillage. All are best container-grown.
Description A tender, moderate to slow-growing evergreen shrub with massed orange summer flowers. Ht up to 6ft (1.8m), Sp 3½ft (1m).
Treatment Best reserved for mild climates when summering outdoors – select a sunny or semi-shaded sheltered spot. Well-lit positions are needed indoors, shaded from midday summer sun. Use strong potting compost. Water freely and mist over in spring and summer, keep barely moist in winter. Provide permanent supports and prune from spring to autumn.
Overwintering Move indoors by mid-September and overwinter at 45–48°F (7–9°C). Don't return outdoors until June – these plants are frost-sensitive.
Propagation Take softwood cuttings in spring and root at 60–65°F (16–18°C).

Glossary

Apical dominance A condition in plants when the growing point of a shoot or stem retards the development of buds immediately below the tip.

Bonemeal A slow-acting organic fertiliser which supplies phosphate and small amounts of nitrogen.

Chlorosis A plant ailment resulting in yellowing of the leaves frequently due to iron deficiency.

Compost Term used to describe a rooting medium for use in pots and other containers – not to be confused with garden compost, which is the end product of decomposed vegetable waste.

Cordon Normally a trained apple or pear with one, two or three straight main stems with short side growths.

Cutting A segment of plant stem, leaf or root used to raise new plants.

Dead-heading The practice of removing faded flower heads.

Die-back A plant condition in which the new shoots die back from the tips.

Espalier A form of wall- or fence-trained tree with pairs of horizontal branches arranged in tiers.

Foliar feeding Application of dilute liquid fertiliser to plant leaves.

Growth regulator A chemical used to promote, retard, or otherwise artificially regulate growth and development.

Iron sequestrene A plant tonic used to prevent or correct iron deficiency.

Knot garden A formal garden made up of series of beds edged with dwarf hedging or similar, enclosing low-growing plants or coloured aggregate. Each bed is separated by paths.

Mulch Traditionally a surface dressing of organic matter applied to the soil around plants. Plastic sheeting is used nowadays.

Parterre An arrangement of one or more formal beds edged around and sub-divided into panels separated by low hedging.

Perennial Strictly any plant which lives for two or more years. The term is often used to describe non-woody-stemmed herbaceous plants.

Pergola Usually an arrangement of arches used to support climbers and other plants.

Pleaching Normally used to describe topiary work on trees having a length of clear stem near ground level.

Rootball The mass of roots and soil or potting compost at the base of a plant.

Scorching Searing and browning or blackening of leaves, shoots, flowers and roots, due to wind, frost, sun or dryness.

Shank A leg or single stem near ground level and carrying a head of branches.

Side-shooting The removal of secondary shoots to prevent branching or forking.

Soakaway A rubble drain to catch surplus water.

Spindle bush A form of vertical single-stemmed cordon, or spindle-like tree, with short side growths.

Stopping The practice of removing the growing point of a plant. This is usually done either to promote branching or to stop further growth.

Suckers Shoots or growths usually arising at or below ground level.

Topiary The art of clipping and training trees and other plants into various shapes, including animals and formal geometric patterns.

Treillage The term used to describe wrought metalwork in the form of arbours and animals, and also the art of training climbers over this framework.

Index